BACK ROADS

D1612580

BACK ROADS

THE STORIES BEHIND SOME OF AUSTRALIA'S MOST
REMARKABLE AND INSPIRING RURAL COMMUNITIES

HEATHER EWART &
KAREN MICHELMORE

ABC
BOOKS

The ABC 'Wave' device is a trademark of the
Australian Broadcasting Corporation and is used
under licence by HarperCollins*Publishers* Australia.

First published in Australia in 2018
by HarperCollins*Publishers* Australia Pty Limited
ABN 36 009 913 517
harpercollins.com.au

Copyright © Australian Broadcasting Corporation 2018

The right of Heather Ewart (foreword) and Karen Michelmore (main text) to be identified
as the authors of this work has been asserted by them in accordance with the *Copyright
Amendment (Moral Rights) Act 2000*.

HarperCollins*Publishers*
Level 13, 201 Elizabeth Street, Sydney NSW 2000, Australia
Unit D1, 63 Apollo Drive, Rosedale, Auckland 0632, New Zealand
A 53, Sector 57, Noida, UP, India
1 London Bridge Street, London SE1 9GF, United Kingdom
2 Bloor Street East, 20th floor, Toronto, Ontario M4W 1A8, Canada
195 Broadway, New York NY 10007, USA

A catalogue record for this book is available from the National Library of Australia

ISBN: 978 0 7333 3968 4 (paperback)
ISBN: 978 1 4607 1084 5 (ebook)

Cover design by Phil Campbell Design
Front cover photo by Karen Michelmore
Back cover photo left by Ron Ekkel features team cameraman Ron Ekkel, executive
producer Brigid Donovan, editor Tony Kuric, presenter Heather Ewart, producer Lisa
Whitehead, supervising producer Kerri Ritchie and series producer Louise Turley; photo
right features Heather Ewart, Ron Ekkel, producer and author Karen Michelmore and sound
engineer John Peterson.
Map by Alex Hotchin
p267: 'Tea' words and music Sam Brown, © 1988. Wayblue Ltd, administered by BMG
Rights Management (UK) Ltd.
Typeset in Sabon LT by Kirby Jones
Printed and bound in Australia by McPhersons Printing Group
The papers used by HarperCollins in the manufacture of this book are a natural, recyclable
product made from wood grown in sustainable plantation forests. The fibre source and
manufacturing processes meet recognised international environmental standards, and carry
certification.

For Fiona Reynolds,
who supported and believed in Back Roads
from the beginning.

Timor Sea

DARWIN

PINE CREEK

INDIAN OCEAN

DERBY

NORTHERN TERRITORY

KARRATHA

WESTERN AUSTRALIA

SOUTH AUSTRALIA

NULLARBOR PLAIN

CEDUNA

PERTH

KATANNING

GREAT AUSTRALIAN BIGHT

SOUTHERN OCEAN

BACK ROADS

Arafura Sea

Gulf of Carpentaria

THURSDAY ISLAND

PACIFIC OCEAN

KARUMBA

GREAT BARRIER REEF

WINTON

MIDDLETON

GREAT

QUEENSLAND

DIVIDING

THALLON

BRISBANE

MARREE

WHITE CLIFFS

NEW SOUTH WALES

RANGE

ADELAIDE

CANBERRA

SYDNEY

MUNDULLA

BIRCHIP

CORRYONG

ROBE

NATIMUK

YACKANDANDAH

HARROW

VIOLET TOWN

MELBOURNE

VICTORIA

BASS STRAIT

TASMANIA

QUEENSTOWN

HOBART

DUNALLEY

CYGNET

Contents

Foreword

by Heather Ewart

I GREW UP ON *back roads*, dirt ones, and so did everyone I knew. They were dry and dusty in summer, wet and boggy in winter and were the only way into or out of our sheep and wheat farm near Murchison in Victoria, close to the Goulburn River. Our large family has lived in these parts since the 1850s. Many of them have never seen any need to move, and those who have always want to come back.

A long, tree-lined gravel driveway led to our place, Murambie Downs, and I can still recall the excitement as a child when our dogs barking would signal a visitor was coming down the track. It might be a wandering swagman – there were still a few around back then – or a travelling salesman in his van packed with all the latest haberdashery and lollies for us kids. In September it would be the shearers, but more often than not it would be friends and neighbours dropping in for a meal or a cuppa. The kettle was always boiling on our kitchen stove and there was always time to share a yarn and a laugh or two.

I was exposed to characters aplenty ... Decent, hardworking men and women who'd had their fair share of good and bad times and personal tragedies on the land, but with a sense of humour as dry as the *back roads* they lived on to carry them through.

Years later, in early 2015, as our small team was formulating the idea of an ABC TV series on life in rural Australia, it struck me that those sorts of characters wouldn't be confined to my community of Murchison. They'd have to be right around the country. And sure enough, they were.

The title *Back Roads* was born and we hit the road with our theme firmly in our minds: you never know who you'll meet or what you'll find when you travel the *back roads*. This was to be a show about the resilience of the bush, and seemingly ordinary country people doing some extraordinary things.

It didn't take long. Our first stop was the small town of Yackandandah on the edge of Victoria's high country, where we met the unforgettable 12-year-old Moira Dale. As she shared scones she'd baked for our afternoon tea with her mother and aunt, Moira calmly explained she had autism but that wasn't going to prevent her from being a good actor. In fact, her career was already off and running, launched in the local production *Scaredy Cat*, which went on to feature in the

Melbourne Comedy Festival to great acclaim. Moira is still acting and has become a cherished friend. That's what can happen on the *back roads*.

From the hills, to the outback, to the sea, we came across one inspiring story after another and many of the characters we remain in touch with. It's been one of the great joys of working on *Back Roads*.

And it doesn't take much for childhood memories to come flooding back either. Like the smell of hot bread fresh out of the oven at Kevin and Gail Sharp's bakery at Birchip in the Mallee – though their real claim to fame is their award-winning vanilla slices.

Like Craig Stinear – or 'Oolie', as the locals call him – in Ceduna, South Australia, whose job is to keep a watchful eye on the road across the Nullarbor and who has the same sort of droll tongue I used to hear around our farm kitchen table. I actually fell for his line that he was setting up in the middle of the highway for an international hopscotch competition.

Like Joan Sinclair near Corryong, in the foothills of the Snowy Mountains, still riding horses in her 80s, and enjoying a camp oven roast with her mates around the fire, just as our family used to on weekend picnics.

Like Lyn the mobile hairdresser in North Queensland and her loyal friend and assistant, Fil, with whom I counted caravans and tall anthills to while away the hours between appointments on our long road trip – a bit like playing I Spy in the car with my siblings in the old days.

Like the brave Gurjit Sondhu at Harrow, whose life was turned upside down when her husband, Tari, died soon after we met them, yet Gurjit is determined to stay put and keep their farm going, just as my mother did after my father died of a heart attack.

No matter which town we go to, the residents seem familiar to me because they have the same traits and way of expressing themselves as those people I grew up with on the *back roads*. They just get on with it, secure in the knowledge that this is the place where they belong.

When we began our journey, we didn't know if we'd get past the first series. We hoped, but couldn't be sure, that viewers would come along with us. Yet they did, in droves. Somehow, we've hit a nerve out there. A way of life many city people may have thought was gone is still there. While filming, we're now constantly approached by travellers telling us they're on their own road trips visiting the towns we've featured. And the towns themselves have reported to us that's meant a boost to their economies, which is such an unexpected and welcome side effect. We hope in some small way we've helped bridge the gap between city and country.

For me, it's been a privilege to showcase the best of country Australia. I've spent most of my career as a political reporter and foreign correspondent and have now come full circle. Clearly the lure of the *back roads* is hard to shake, as you'll discover in the pages of this book.

– Heather Ewart

1

Yackandandah

Location: 308 km north-east of Melbourne, Victoria.

Population: 1811

Aired: Yackandandah was the first town *Back Roads* visited when it first got the go-ahead for an initial eight-episode series in early 2015. It aired in mid-December 2015 – and the town's folk festival has been booked out ever since.

> *And it goes like this ... F-o-r-m bananas, form-form*
> *bananas.*
> *And pe-e-el bananas, peel-peel bananas.*

A POD OF A dozen or so kids in socked feet and colourful T-shirts and shorts is standing in a circle inside Yackandandah Public Hall. Their arms are flailing about in rhythm with their words as they create giant invisible bananas in the air and then exuberantly strip off the skins with long, fluid motions.

Piles of muddy football shoes lie abandoned in the doorway – they're mostly boys here today, and they've just rushed over from practice.

The Banana Song is a favourite warm-up and has already proven its worth under the tutelage of chief fruit herder and drama teacher Brendan Hogan.

'That's just a funny little warm-up game to get the kids in the mood for being stupid,' he explains.

It's 2015 and the *Back Roads* crew is here to film with the drama group, the Yackandandah Young Players. The kids have become something of a celebrity troupe among residents in their hometown of Yackandandah, a picturesque hamlet in the foothills of Victoria's high country.

Just a few weeks ago they were performing their play *Scaredy Cat* to packed audiences in the Big Smoke, in the Spiegeltent at Melbourne's International Comedy Festival.

'That was our little ritual before we went on – we used to sing that song and that would get us all geared up for the stage,' Brendan says.

And … go bananas, go-go bananas.

The group starts dance-jogging on the spot.

One student is stomping around particularly enthusiastically. Moira Dale is 12, and was a hit on the Melbourne comedy circuit as a charming and funny French-horn-playing little trooper called Kowalski, a part written especially for her by Brendan. She doesn't know it, but she'll also soon win the hearts of the *Back Roads* audience for her frank and refreshing view of the world.

Moira has straight straw-coloured hair which frames her wide-grinning face, complete with a thick fringe. She loves wearing brightly coloured clothes with bold patterns.

'She's the star of the show,' Brendan says of his young protégé. 'She steals every scene that she's in.'

Moira joined the Yackandandah acting crew soon after the group formed in 2013. Brendan started the drama classes because he loves the arts, and it seemed like a natural progression from the quirky historical short films he wrote and directed the kids in when he was a teacher at Yackandandah Primary School a few years earlier. He'd been poached to become the principal of another school, but still lived in Yackandandah with his partner, Stacey. It was hard to leave.

Brendan says the classes started with just a dozen kids for an hour a week – everybody was welcome to join. 'Within about 12 months we had 45 kids who were signed up and doing it, and we were running three classes. And drama, along with football and netball and hockey and horse-riding, became a cool thing to do.'

The classes are fun and inclusive – and all centred around comedy.

'Kids who are 12 are quite inspirational in their comedy,' Brendan explains. They want it to have a bit more of an edge, and so it became pretty clear to me that it was going to have to be a play written specifically for those kids, so that every kid in the group could succeed, because some kids were stronger than others.'

Among those with a strong, unique stage presence was Moira. Her mother, Rebecca Gowan, a local GP, had emailed Brendan shortly after the group began, asking if Moira could take part. But there was something troubling on Moira's mind when she joined the group. She pulled her teacher aside on her first day.

He remembers, 'She said, "Brendan, there's something I need to tell you before we start. I've got Asperger's, but you need to know it won't make a difference."'

Moira had only recently been diagnosed with autism spectrum disorder. She thought it was important people close to her knew about the condition, and she still does, 'in case they were wondering why I was doing something in a certain way'.

'I just might do things differently,' she continues. 'Like, it doesn't make me completely different. I'm still a person with four limbs, if that makes sense; four limbs and a head.'

Brendan says it made absolutely no difference to the group. Except for one thing: he rewrote the script for *Scaredy Cat* with a special new part.

'Someone who marches to the beat of their own drum, and is very endearing and disarming – that was written just for Moira,' Brendan says.

Moira seized the role and ran with it.

Rebecca says Moira's always loved performing – it was the family's way of entertaining itself.

'We used to do a lot of dancing with scarves; just mad Mum stuff that you do. I also think living out in the country, you just don't want to be schlepping in and out to town the whole time. Making your own fun because you live on a farm type-of-stuff.

'We'd have musical concerts with the family; people would get up and sing every Christmas, probably in the week before Christmas. You were expected to get up and sing a song or play a musical instrument – not in a formal way; you could tell a poem, do a full skit. Moira would have just stood up when she was two or three and belted out a song which was completely off key, in a little pink tutu.'

But the work with the drama club has really brought something extra out in Moira.

'She's blossomed; she's come out,' Rebecca says. 'The drama's been fantastic but also the friendships, and the kids are really accepting of each other. *Scaredy Cat* was massive. Any little girl loves the spotlight, I think, and she was fortunate enough to be in a community like Yackandandah that gave her that opportunity.'

It's 2018 and we're sitting around a wooden table in the family kitchen. Moira's colourful artwork adorns the walls.

Moira's father, Gregory, is on the phone to her 17-year-old brother, Fergus, who's away on a gap year. Moira, now 15, is taking me through the details of her acting CV, reflecting on her achievements, with several digressions to interesting memories.

She likes doing comedy, but laments that no one else really does comedy for kids.

'There's comedy for kids, but it's, like, adults,' she says. 'There's not actual kids in it.

'I like comedy, I like acting, drama. I like being another person, and I like doing that because a lot of the time I'm just me, and I don't know how to be a different person. Brendan [Hogan] gave me that structure, of what the person was like, and then I was able to develop it. Within that I can make it my own thing.'

After *Scaredy Cat* came *Caged Canary* in 2016 – another role written by Brendan Hogan especially for Moira – this time a tough, tattooed, tobacco-loving orphan called Peaches. Another unlikely comedy, it was set in the ravages of World War II Germany.

'I smoked, I had tattoos – they were just sleeves, you know; you can get fake tattoo sleeves,' Moira explains. 'It felt weird, because I'd never do that in real life because, you know, it's bad. Literally, in the end, bad for you.'

Moira is continuing with drama classes at her high school.

Her family lives in a green weatherboard house in Indigo Valley, amid rolling golden-coloured hills about eight minutes' drive north of Yackandandah. She's surrounded in these parts by family: Moira is one of 35 cousins. There's three generations of relatives in the local cemetery.

A long driveway lined with gum trees leads up to the house and it's quiet and idyllic. Rebecca grew up on the property, Yarrandoo, with her 12 brothers and sisters. It's where the family gathered to watch Moira's foray onto the national stage in 2015 with her appearance on *Back Roads*.

'We didn't know what was about to hit us, did we, Moira?' Rebecca laughs.

She's not just talking about the wave of affection for Moira for speaking frankly and with humour about autism, and the national conversations it engendered. That was soon forgotten by the family – although temporarily – after the episode aired.

Fire was raging across the Indigo Valley. It was Sunday 20 December 2015 – a week after the television broadcast. Moira had evacuated with her mother. Her father, Gregory, stayed behind to fight the blaze.

'It burned about 95 per cent of our farm,' Moira states. 'We brought the dogs in. The chooks were saved. The garden was saved. The house was saved. All the time I was thinking, Dad, don't die, and don't let the house burn down.'

Gregory adds, 'I would have had a bit of explaining to do, wouldn't I?'

There are few signs of it now as pink hues descend over the dry, rolling hills as the sun sets in. There's a dam surrounded by gum trees a few hundred metres away. Closer still are about a dozen large raised beds covered with netting.

Moira and her mother ritually pick bountiful passionfruit from a large, generous and unwieldy vine. There's a short but plentiful harvest of plums in early summer, and then the peaches ripen. Daily they visit the chickens in their pen overlooking the valley, bearing the gift of a bucket of orange peel and food scraps. It's all part of the family routine, as is Moira's afternoon swim as soon as she arrives home from school.

As well as drama classes, Moira also loves cooking and craft. She's excited to start her own herb and vegetable patch in one of the planter boxes.

'I just like growing produce – usually it's just been Mum's garden and me helping her, but this year we have garden beds out there, so when one of them finishes, Mum's going to give that to me to plant my own stuff in,' she says. 'I want carrots, and then in the pots I'll have stuff like parsley, sage, rosemary and thyme.'

One of Moira's charms is that she knows exactly what she wants, and can clearly enunciate her reasons for wanting it. She dreams of one day opening a cafe selling cakes, and craft, in Yackandandah.

'Because that's all stuff that I like doing,' she explains.

There are many hints to Moira's autism. Her mother says she has a memory for detail, and would be a great cheese-taster, such is her sense of smell. Sometimes, though, for Moira, the perceived smells can be overwhelming.

Like many teenagers she has anxiety, but with her autism, it's more about experiencing intense sensations, like feeling she has sticky hands, even though her hands are clean.

She also loves maps: following the details of the lines of the road, and the patterns of different landmarks and parks.

'I'm interested in where roads go – where they start and where they end,' Moira says. 'You might go left, right, around, up, down, left, right for about 200 kilometres and you'll end up in Sydney, let's say. There will be intersections. Some roads might end but other roads start. It's like when one door closes another one opens.'

Moira was diagnosed with autism spectrum disorder in 2012 when she was ten. Before she appeared on *Back Roads*, she didn't really like discussing it all that much. She wavered before she was due to do the filming, until host Heather Ewart sat Moira down and in her matter-of-fact way explained that she knew a lot of people with autism. It was perfectly normal. Except, until then, people didn't really talk about it. Not on television, anyway.

'Before *Back Roads*, I didn't really want to talk about it unless I felt really, really, really safe with somebody,' Moira says. 'Because I wanted to keep it kind of private.'

After the episode aired, Moira received huge positive affirmation, and a wave of affection from across Australia. She now doesn't mind talking about her condition – especially, she says, if it will help others understand.

'Well, I got diagnosed in … what year was it, Mum?'

'In 2012,' says Rebecca.

'She's better with dates than I am,' Moira says quietly.

Moira remembers early questions about whether she had autism were dismissed because she didn't tick all the boxes of the condition. She was a great communicator, for example.

For her mother, Rebecca, the nine-year journey to a diagnosis was a struggle for answers. It started when she first took Moira to a GP when she hadn't started walking by 18 months.

'She didn't walk until late because she was very floppy, so we took her to quite a few different specialists. I kept saying I think something is going on but they just dismissed me as a worried mum.'

In hindsight, the signs were obvious.

'Being a GP, people come in with these forms for disability and you have to tick the boxes, and I'd be thinking, Moira does that: she doesn't like her hair being brushed, she can't stand haircuts, doesn't like certain strong smells. If anyone's a smoker, oh my God, she hates smokers.

'There probably would have been ten health professionals that she saw before she was diagnosed: two occupational therapists, a speech therapist, neurologists. But no one put anything together. People would say she doesn't have autism – she looks you in the eye and she talks to you.'

Moira has incredible verbal skills for her age. Rebecca says she'd make an amazing lawyer. Even as a young kid, Moira would walk up to anybody in town and start chatting. Being part of a family where everyone was encouraged to have an opinion no doubt helped. She's been a member of the town's local choir since she was four.

'I'm a real extrovert, as you can probably tell,' Moira says. 'A lot of autistic people can be introverts. So that didn't match.'

Moira reels off a list of other potential characteristics of autism she doesn't hold, such as excelling at maths, or being obsessed with cars or computers.

'Well, I obviously don't tick I'm a male. I'm not an introvert. I know a bit about cars but not so much – for cars it's kind of a half tick, half cross.'

She sometimes struggles to read people's facial expressions.

'If you felt embarrassed and it was coming out on your face as embarrassed, I might misinterpret it as angry.'

Moira explains she also sees the world differently. In shapes and patterns. She will see love hearts in the spurs of trees, or in rocks.

Finally, when Moira was ten, Rebecca took her back to the pediatrician and told the doctor firmly that she believed Moira had autism. The pediatrician sent them to a specialist in Melbourne.

'Within about an hour I said, "What do you reckon?" and she said, "Well, of course she's got autism," Rebecca recalls. 'And I said, "Oh." But it was a real shock.'

The diagnosis – while a long time coming – was a stark revelation. And a relief.

'It was validation as a parent. You think something's not quite right, and are searching, searching for answers and not really getting anywhere. And then you go to the expert who just validates it. So you're not going mad.'

Moira says things made a lot more sense once she was diagnosed.

'They're like, oh, that's why she does so and so,' Moira says. 'I need more time to do a lot of things than other people would. Like, my bus in the morning leaves at eight o'clock. I wake up at 6.30, but some people would be able to wake up at a quarter past seven and get ready [in time], but I needed to wake up that little bit earlier.'

But Rebecca adds that not everyone saw it that way. She had people telling her that Moira shouldn't be labelled.

'I said hang on, hang on – labelling can actually be quite useful. Now we know why she takes forever to wrap up. Now we know why she can't write very well. Labels don't define you but they can help you cut someone a bit of slack.

'I don't think it really changes who Moira is or what she is. I mean, we don't think that and most of the community know Moira for who she is, and that's the really good thing about the community as a whole; they just accept people for who they are.

'They see Moira as a quirky kid. Even when she was little, when she was three or four, everyone in Yackandandah knew her and they still know her now.'

And if there's anyone ever unlikely to be limited by a label, it's Moira.

Life can be tough – she's had some difficulties with learning but is lucky enough to have a support team at her high school.

Rebecca says her daughter's appearance on *Back Roads* helped others recognise the signs in their own families, and start conversations. 'I know that it did have a bit of a ripple effect of social acceptance. I didn't expect that going in.'

Rebecca notes that girls with autism are often misdiagnosed, although more is beginning to be understood about how autism presents in girls.

'I'd like to think they'd pick it up a little bit quicker now,' Rebecca says, adding that her daughter's diagnosis helped her pick up the clues in her own general practice.

And acting might come so naturally for Moira because of her condition, she suggests.

'Part of the way that girls with autism are, they have to act on being normal,' Rebecca notes. 'That's why there's quite a few actors who have autism, because they are used to acting their whole life. We did a lot of social skills training, so that when you see someone to try and be like a social detective ... but she has to act every day.'

Moira feels she's gained a lot through her drama classes: 'It's definitely given me the ability to be myself, even though I'm playing other people. And I like doing it; I've found something that I like doing but I don't really have to put in any effort for, apart from remembering a few lines.'

Sounds like the perfect combination.

Note: Lyrics from 'The Banana Song (aka Guacamole Song)' reproduced with permission of Dr Jean Feldman (drjean.org).

2
Violet Town

Location: 181 km north of Melbourne.

Population: 874

Aired: *Back Roads* visited Violet Town in November 2017 and it was the final episode of the third season of the show, broadcast in January 2018.

DIANE REEVES BOUGHT A big-wheeled, full-of-throttle trike motorcycle when her father died. A big, gleaming, glossy, head-turning blue trike.

'Skinflintin' old bastard,' she says in a thick Australian drawl. 'We blew the lot. Blew all his money on a trike and we knew he would hate it.'

Diane's father died in 2007 at the age of 103. Oliver Reeves' actions in life had a powerful impact. But his death – and the inheritance it presented – enabled the cathartic purchase of the trike, and finally kickstarted Diane's brave, slow journey to self-acceptance.

As is the case with many of life's stories, Diane has now ended up exactly where she needs to be. Diane and Linda have been living in their modest Violet Town home, about two hours drive north of Melbourne, for a decade. They've been a couple for more than 37 years.

Until just a few years ago, Diane was known by all and sundry as David Reeves – Dave the shearer, the blacksmith, the welder and truck driver. To the outside world, a pretty macho bloke.

'Everything I've done has been super-male to try and hide who I am,' Diane explains.

It's only been a handful of years – since 2015 – that Diane's had the courage to present her true self to the world. As a woman. The first time she did, she was 64. She came out at a gathering of blokey trike enthusiasts. Diane is transgender. She says she feels about 80 per cent female.

'It's a fact that I don't fit; I don't pass as female,' she says. 'I'm six foot five, I weigh 108 kilos and I've got a big old male carcass.'

But Diane can't help the way she feels. She knows that for a fact because she's tortured herself trying to do that very thing for six decades. Since the earliest cravings of childhood, in fact, when as a young boy she was instructed never to touch her sister's brightly coloured clothes and ribbons ever again. It's one of her earliest memories.

'I got a bit of a belting once for wearing a little tutu,' Diane says. 'I loved this little tutu and I got a belting for wearing it and I couldn't understand why. 'Why? What was the deal? "Boys don't do that."'

David Reeves was born on a soldier settlement block near Finley in the lower Riverina in New South Wales, to his father, Oliver, and mother, Edith. He had an older sister, Fran.

Oliver and Edith married during World War II, shortly before Oliver boarded a ship and headed to the conflict in the Middle East, and later Papua New Guinea. When he returned, he ruled his family with a strong fist.

'If tea wasn't on the table at six o'clock, Mum was in trouble,' Diane says.

Her father wasn't much of a farmer, Diane adds, but her parents made a go of it for 13 years – one year longer than they had to under the settlement deal with the government.

'The old man was allocated it, virtually four pegs in a paddock and an irrigation channel, and there you are: make something of it,' Diane recalls. 'It was a lottery system; some people got them, some didn't.

It was where David learned about the world, and his place in it. 'At that stage I didn't know what male and female were. I was just a little kid. It was a bit of a realisation: Oh. Well, there's something that I'm not allowed to do, that I want to do. I was thinking: Why can't I? Why have I got to do this when I want to play with my sister's dolls?'

David didn't fight the rules, but it was a lonely time.

'Mum was very worried about what the neighbours might think and the old man was just the old man. A bit of a nasty character. At that age, say four or five, you tried to please your parents. You take that as gospel. And that's what you did. You take it no further.'

The craving was always there, though: David loved women's clothing – the fabrics and the colours. Every Thursday he would walk past the dress shop in Finley after they'd changed the clothing on the mannequins in the window display.

'I used to walk down the street of a Thursday, across the road, and not look directly at the shop but walk down and see what was in the window. I'd do that every Thursday – but I wouldn't walk on that side of the road in case somebody noticed me looking in the window.'

He never went inside.

'Christ, no. Terrified of that.'

Over the years, David shrank further into himself.

'As time went on, it became obvious that I didn't fit the mould that was set for me. I didn't want to play football. Being as tall as I was, of course, it was, what's wrong with you?

"Are you a girl?" was the comment I used to get and [I'd think]: oh, shit, somebody's figured it out. And I began to hide that part of me, and that started from right back, very early. I'm not allowed to do that, so I'll keep away from that as best I can.'

David spent a lot of time by himself, trapping rabbits around the farm. It was the only time he felt he could be himself.

'I'd go off in the morning and not come back until dark,' Diane reflects. 'I had to be home before the sun went down. That was the rule. And I used to make it most times, but I used to get in trouble if I was out after dark.

'As I got older, the impulses were stronger, so therefore the feelings to keep away from that were even stronger, you know. And that's when this whole "male thing" started.'

David bought an old car, which he built up and supercharged. Then a truck.

'Because then I was a truckie, and truckies don't wear dresses.'

His ideal job when he was a kid was the men who used to grade the remote country roads.

'In New South Wales the grader drivers used to head off on Monday morning with their caravan behind the grader and then a fuel tanker behind that, and they'd disappear into the bush for a week. You wouldn't see them again, and I thought that was a wonderful job. You could be yourself; you could be who you liked. If you wanted to wear a skirt, you could. Nobody would see you. You're on your own. And I thought that was pretty good.'

School wasn't an option. As a result, David didn't learn to read or write until he was in his thirties.

'There was always something to do on the farm. I went to school a bit but there was no continuity. I got to the stage where I'd just keep my head down and keep out of it.'

It meant he didn't learn about transgender people and gender identification issues until much later. As far as he knew, he was the only person feeling this way, hiding a dark secret.

'I didn't have information – I had no idea what the word "transgender" was. Never used it. Never knew what it was. I had no idea of anything, really. It was just a black hole.'

His father was a constant looming presence.

At this time, in mid-1960s rural New South Wales, if you lost your labourer's job in the morning, you'd have another one by the afternoon.

'Somebody would hear you were out of work and they'd be knocking on your door – "Do you want a job?"'

'Little did I know – I only found out very recently – that the old man would follow me around to those jobs and say to the people who were employing me, "Watch that boy, he's strange. Oh, he's weird."'

As much as David was trying to supress his feminine side, his father could sense something. He would search his room for female clothes when David wasn't home.

'He told me, "There's no poofters in the army. When we were in the army there was never any poofters – the blokes soon belted that out of them." And that was his attitude. The way to beat this was to beat it out of you. He never touched me, only to belt me. He never hugged me. And I never touched him. When I was 14 my father told me, "Never shoot yourself with a .22. You won't kill yourself – you might only wound yourself." So when I was 15, I bought a .303. A couple of times it got a bit close but then I had someone to think about and you don't do that sort of thing.'

Diane kept the weapon until the couple moved to Violet Town in 2007.

Violet Town is a quiet place, loosely centred on Honeysuckle Creek and a railway station, and just tucked off the Hume Freeway. Like the town, most of the streets are named after flowers.

Large windows line one side of Diane and Linda's lounge room, allowing light to spill on the dozens of photographs hanging on the wall. They present a record of the couple's life together – on holidays touring Australia, on the trike, and old photos from another life. Of Diane, back when she was David, smiling, short-haired in wide Akubra with long dark shirt and jeans. He's propped next to a big old rusty-looking truck.

On the lounge, a tabby cat with long white whiskers and paws lounges on a red cushion, gazing inquisitively up at the couple.

Today Diane's wearing her blonde hair out, with a splash of pink leopard print and red-framed glasses. Clothes have always been Diane's thing.

Diane never felt close to her mother, who always stood by her father. No matter what. If those walls had come down, they might have found much in common. Edith Reeves was a beautiful dressmaker, and shared Diane's love of fabric and clothes.

After she died in 1997, Diane learned she'd been saving much of her life to leave Oliver, even when she was older and suffering dementia.

'Mum put money away to leave him. She put it away for years and years and years,' Diane says. 'We found $15,000 in every nook and cranny in Mum's bedroom. There was a bag full of old notes, and they were old denomination notes too, some of the old money right up to the modern-day stuff. And in her later years she couldn't remember why she was putting money away, but she was still putting it away.'

But she never left him.

'You didn't do that sort of thing. She was a good Catholic girl. She never went to church but I think that was part of it. And fear of the unknown. And fear of what the neighbours might say. She was very conscious of that. She accepted it and that's what you did in those days.'

Just as David had done, for all those years.

After coming and going from home as a roving shearer, David finally left home for good when he got married at 21 as he tried to live a 'normal' life.

'This is what you did – "21, bloody hell I'd better get married soon".'

David didn't tell his first wife about his internal struggle, and the marriage didn't last.

'I did the thing that all transgender people do: right, I'm married. Purge all your clothes. Throw them out. That's it, I'm not doing that any more. That's the end of it. And three months later you buy something. And something else turns up so you grab a hold of that.'

Diane says for most of her male life, the wardrobe David presented to the world consisted of two pairs of jeans, three shirts and a pair of Blundstone boots. Dressing up in private was a step David could take towards being Diane.

'And I used to take it,' she said. 'It was a recognition: I am who I am.'

Diane loves dressing up – but it's more about being herself, presenting the feminine side for all to see. Even the way she speaks has changed.

'I've dropped the big male macho speech,' she says. 'Because I don't have to anymore. And that's a hell of a relief.'

Even so, her wardrobes are bursting, full of bright patterns.

'It's actually got a little bit out of hand, all the stuff here,' she says, laughing. 'This has grown over the last couple of years, fairly dramatically.'

Her bedroom is painted pink, and ten glossy wigs – brown, blonde and rainbow – hang from a shelf.

'The short blonde ones get worn the most,' Diane says.

And the shoes. All bought online.

'You can't buy size 13 wide in the local shoe shop,' Diane points out.

'The more confidence I get, the more confidence it seems to give people around me, which makes it easier for me again,' Diane says. 'So it's a building stage. They call me Lady Di on occasions because I always overdress – I'm notorious for overdressing. But I've got 60 years to catch up on these girls, so I do overdress – and I know I overdress, but that's why I've got the cupboard full of clothes.'

Diane got invited to a women's group in 2015, soon after coming out. It was a show-and-tell afternoon.

'One lady brought along a few plants to show and another brought her mosaics, and hidden out the back is me, dressed to the nines.'

The friend who invited her told the group about transgender people and then introduced Diane.

'And I walked out and jaws hit the floor. It ended up a really nice afternoon. It was very pleasant. There was no animosity, no bitterness, no nastiness because I had a member of that community on my side to start with. I think it was the old peer group pressure working: everybody sat up and was great and they actually asked me to join. I was really thrilled at that.'

Linda describes the public blossoming of Diane as like having a teenage girl in the house, 'only a bit more expensive'.

Things started to change for Diane when she met Linda, almost four decades ago, through a theatre group in Bright, Victoria.

'I saw her walking down the street. Linda had her hair to her bum, had a batik wraparound skirt – remember the old wraparound long skirts? – and sandals, and a bag with tassels. The perfect hippy. She really did look the perfect hippy. And I thought: gee, she looks all right.'

They got to know each other, and by their second date Diane, then David, had confided in Linda. 'I said to Linda I was transgender and told her right back then because I didn't want to go through all that again.'

It was a second marriage for both of them. And it's proven the test of time. They've been together 37 years and counting.

'The second date, Di said, you know I'm a transvestite – which was what they were called back then,' Linda says. 'And I said, oh yeah, rightio. You seem very nice. It doesn't worry me. I've heard about them. That was fine, quite fine. So obviously we kept going. So, yeah, I've known all along.

'I just have known Di ... for years and inside she's no different. She's still that same warm, generous person and, you know, we just need to keep her going and feeling herself.'

The couple married in 1985 and built a mudbrick house together in beautiful Porepunkah, in the shadow of Victoria's Mount Buffalo. David had a welding business, and they both enjoyed competing in dressage. They spent seven years there, before moving 40 kilometres north to bigger acreage at Mudgegonga.

'We called it the Four-R Farm, which stood for rocks, roos, rabbits and Reeves, and that's just not about far wrong,' Diane says. 'So we removed the rabbits, relocated the roos and rolled the rocks. It was a fresh start for us.'

They developed the farm for 15 years, and became part of the community. David was the fire brigade captain for more than a decade.

But still David kept his secret hidden.

They sold up and bought a caravan, and travelled around Australia. Eventually they ended up in Violet Town. It was halfway between Linda's kids and her parents. The housing was affordable. And there was a train station nearby.

Over ten years it turned into home and a place Diane felt comfortable enough to take the first steps towards self-acceptance.

The death of her father spurred on the final result.

With the purchase of the shiny new toy, the couple embraced all things trike. They were enmeshed in a club for enthusiasts. David was on the committee and Linda was the secretary. They put in plenty of hours and organised rides.

Until things turned sour in 2015, when two warring factions of the club committee were on edge. David and Linda found themselves booted off the board because others were concerned their married status might lead them to work together and influence votes. It came as a huge shock to the couple.

'I was feeling a bit thrown out, a little bit,' Diane recalls. 'The amount of work that we'd put into that, and the angst. We lost a lot of bloody sleep.'

Diane wanted to give them something to really think about, so she talked to Linda about it, and then publicly outed herself.

'Did you know I'm transgender?' she asked club members gathered in a hotel in Albury, New South Wales.

Linda says, 'There was discrimination against us because we were a married couple and Di just decided, right, I'll give them something to discriminate against! So she actually came out and that event set off all of this.

'For me, that negative event was the best thing that ever happened because there's no hiding. We used to have an alarm on the front gate and things like that, but that doesn't happen now.'

Diane then rang around some friends who weren't at the gathering, and confided the news to them 'to soften the blow'.

'We went from there. And survived.'

A few weeks later, Diane made her first public outing, dressed up, for the 2015 Bendigo Easter Festival Gala Parade. A photo captures the trike decorated in sets of bunny ears and pink, green and red paper lanterns.

Diane, in the driver's seat, is giving two thumbs up to the camera, looking nervous but with a genuine smile. She's dressed in a pink fairy skirt and matching high heels, and a brown wig peeps out beneath her blue helmet topped with bunny ears. Linda sits behind her, grinning but slightly uncertain, as if bracing for the unknown journey ahead.

'It was an easy way to do it because I wasn't coming out as female – I was getting all dressed up in fancy clothes; it was an Easter parade,' Diane says. 'All the trikes are decorated so I decorated myself up. Ever tried riding a trike with six-inch heels? Not a good idea.'

The trike enthusiasts had arranged to eat dinner together at a restaurant. 'We were a bit late getting there because of me – I was dressed to the nines,' Diane recalls. 'Make-up, heels, the works. And I walked in and they applauded. I started crying. It was a good night.

'After it, of course, I took everything off. Put on a nice skirt and low heels and we sat there until one o'clock in the morning. I was just part of the furniture. People were asking questions, which was lovely.

'They were fine with it, which started the feeling of acceptance, and my self-esteem was built up a little bit. And the more people I've told, the better that's got. If you've got confidence in yourself it makes a difference to other people around you. They feed off that and accept it.'

Coming out in Violet Town was a little trickier. Diane was trying to ease into it by switching between Diane and David. But it just confused people.

'Cold turkey's better,' she says.

Diane's gaining confidence every day. The appearance on *Back Roads* did wonders, she reckons, although she was 'shitting bricks' before it went to air. She's now officially changed her birth certificate to Diane, and she's started speaking out on issues that affect transgender people, like accessing public restrooms. Even now, Diane still feels self-conscious going into the ladies' toilet and will use a disabled toilet if there is one, because they are unisex.

'They're putting a new toilet in here and I wrote to the VTAG [Violet Town Action Group] committee and said, how about you make a section of that gender-neutral?' she says. 'They took it on board, which I was really pleased about.'

More than anything, Diane loves being one of the girls: 'It's just so nice to be accepted for who you are,' she says. 'Probably the first time I've ever belonged anywhere is here.'

Shortly after filming *Back Roads*, Diane and Linda sold their blue trike.

'The guy rode out the gate and I thought, that's a part of my life gone,' Diane remembers. 'I'm surprised it didn't affect me much at all.'

Looking back on the past 60 years of keeping herself hidden, Diane describes her feelings as 'double-edged'.

'I had a reasonable childhood because I didn't know any better,' she explains. 'I think I was born too early. I would have been better off born, say, 20 years ago, when this transgender thing was becoming fairly acceptable.

'That said,' Diane adds, 'I wouldn't have missed Linda and our years together for anything. That's been a big part of my life and I wouldn't have missed it.'

3

Birchip

Location: 311 km north-west of Melbourne.

Population: 702

Aired: Birchip was one of the first towns *Back Roads* visited in its first season in 2015. The episode aired in December of that year.

TWO MEN ARE HUDDLED closely together, clipboards in hand, surveying the plate of food before them. To the untrained observer, it looks exactly the same as the dozens of other plates stretching out in both directions along the long narrow table. Six neatly cut vanilla slices with gleaming tops, each engorged with luscious thick custard, stare back at them.

Bright yellow tickets containing a number are folded in half along the row, each belonging to one anonymous, hopeful baker and listing the competing class: professional.

It's the 2015 annual Great Australian Vanilla Slice Triumph in Merbein, Victoria, about six hours' drive north of Melbourne. *Back Roads* has followed baker Kevin Sharp and his wife Gail from their Birchip bakery in Victoria's Mallee region to the competition. The couple are stalwarts of the vanilla slice game. They've won the competition three times already. But each win doesn't diminish the hunger for victory – it only makes the craving stronger. Success in 2015 would mean the world to Kevin.

'I'm pretty nervous,' he says. 'It means a fair bit to me. We are forever trying to improve it – that's the key to it. They're all trying to knock us off.'

Competition is tough and expectations high.

Inside the judging marquee, the official pokes the top of the neat slice with his little finger, and starts dabbing at the thick white icing.

'The fondant looks very good,' he says in a hushed voice. 'That's been done very well.'

Both judges are dressed in chef's whites, with smart black piping around the trims, and a row of round little black buttons down their fronts. They are wearing matching white caps. And nodding in unison.

'They've tempered that fondant superbly,' notes the other man. 'Balance is good. It's not a bad industry-standard vanilla slice.'

By day's end the five judges will have tasted dozens of vanilla slices. It's a day of high stakes sugar – not just for the judges, but for the bakers from around Australia who enter each year. Winning, or even placing, has a huge impact.

For Birchip, sales of vanilla slices have skyrocketed from 2500 a year to more than 30,000. People will go hours out of their way to buy them – and even order them in advance if they are passing through.

'On Friday, I've got a bloke coming through from Mildura at 8.30am – he wants four,' Kevin says.

Importantly, the customers might also call in at the local newsagent, or the gift shop next door, and buy something, helping to keep the town afloat. Birchip has also stopped its decline in population.

'I'm not saying vanilla slice made people want to live in town, but it certainly had a role,' says Gail.

Gail is heavily involved in the Birchip community – she drives the local ambulance and has even delivered a baby or two. She says the people of Birchip care about each other – which is why it's such a strong community.

'If I don't see an elderly gentlemen, one of the regulars, in the shop for three days, I know that's not right,' Gail says. 'So I'll go and knock on a door, and other people are like that too.

'It's a neighbour looking at a nature strip and knowing you, a 70- or 80-year-old woman, is not going to get out a lot, and they'll go and mow it for you. It's basic morals. Australian morals and care, and I'm proud of it.'

Then Gail confides a secret. Unlike Kevin, she's actually not a huge fan of vanilla slice.

'It's never been a favourite cake of mine. But I have learned how important it is,' she says.

'I'm more about heart and soul, and kids and community. As long as we are eating, drinking, and we live in a beautiful house – that's what this community has done for us. We've managed to bring up four kids. I don't care if that's [through] meat pies or vanilla slices.'

Today it is the humble vanilla slice that is being celebrated. The competition in Merbein has developed into a vanilla slice festival of sorts.

Red, pink and yellow balloons float effortlessly, alongside tin rattlers selling raffle tickets and stalls upon stalls offering up, for $3, freshly baked vanilla slices in shades of pink, chocolate and white, set in individual plastic trays. There's even a song, composed by students at the local Merbein P-10 College.

'Vanilla slice is yum-my,' the young woman Bec Griffiths sings from the temporary stage, backed by guitarist Joshua Hudson.

It's even better in my tum-my.
There's icing. And sug-ar. Biscuit and coconut too.
We got it.
You want it.
Vanilla slice for every-one.

Of course, Kevin won't allow himself to be distracted today. Of all days. He's got his eye focused on the top prize.

'I think I want to prove myself. To myself. And my family,' he says quietly.

Of course, Kevin has nothing to prove. To anyone.

Kevin has invested ten years into perfecting his version of the humble vanilla slice. Every time he tries and doesn't win, he corners the experts to find out why.

'Kevin is just fastidious in wanting to produce the quality,' Gail says proudly. 'Every time we have entered the competition, he's quizzed the judges as to why he has scored poorly or scored well, and what the difference was between him and his competitors, and finally we got to a first prize, after a third and a second.'

Kevin says he works at improving both his recipes and techniques.

'I thought it was a pretty good vanilla slice when I entered the first year, but I don't know – if I produced it now, I would throw it in the bin,' he says. 'That's how much we've improved the product.

'That's one of the reasons I started entering, to put myself up against them and see how far I was behind, or how far in front, or where I was. Where I sat. And to try to improve it. That's what it's done for me.'

Back in Birchip, it's hard to miss Sharp's Bakery. It's just in front of the big red statue the town has become famous for – Birchip's Mallee Bull.

The window of the shop proudly proclaims the past wins, and inside, tucked on a shelf, a row of gleaming trophies line the wall. The first win was in 2009.

'I was nearly on another planet – it actually took a while to sink in,' Gail remembers. 'We both teared up.'

Kevin says people started turning up earlier than that – back when they were placing third.

'I don't think I realised then; I didn't realise what an impact it could have,' he says.

Gail says it's mostly people travelling through who buy the slices.

'People just travel – if they are within an hour or two hours, they will drop in and hopefully we have got them,' she says. 'With six or seven hundred people in Birchip they can't eat 150 vanilla slices every day, so there is lots of passing traffic on the Sunraysia Highway each day, heading from Ballarat to Mildura.'

Kevin and Gail bought the bakery as newlyweds in 1977. That was forty-one years ago. They met when they were 15 in Merbein, Kevin's home town, notably, where the Great Australian Vanilla Slice Triumph is being held this year, in 2015.

Kevin was being raised by his mother, who owned a milk bar in town. His father had been a bread carter for a local bakery, but died in an accident at a winery when Kevin was nine. The bakery was where Kevin got his first job in the industry.

Gail had been sent to Merbein to learn typing and was staying at a boarding house, right opposite the milk bar.

'The first night I was there, I looked across the road and I thought, who's that?' Gail recalls. 'He was this long-haired lout. I went over and bought a Drumstick.'

They were engaged three years later at 18. Married at 21.

'Kevin said, "I want to own our own business,"' says Gail, who had thrown in typing to become a nurse by then. 'I thought, that sounds great. So I gave up nursing at $30 an hour to work at $7 an hour as a baker's wife.'

The couple drove around the region looking at bakeries that were for sale.

'One was falling down and the other one needed $200,000 to rejuvenate it,' Gail notes.

Then they called in to Birchip one Saturday morning to buy a pie. They liked it straight away so asked the owners outright if it was for sale. It wasn't.

'We were so blessed because here was this Dutch couple who had been there for 22 years without a holiday,' Gail says. 'They said no, it's not for sale, but give us your phone number. So we went home. Within a week we had a phone call to say this is the price. Yes, it's for sale. Are you interested?

'So even down to that, we couldn't raise the finance. But the bank manager in Merbein went on holidays. Kevin's stepfather's best mate was the temporary bank manager – we got the loan. Kevin's mother had to mortgage her house and we bought the bakery.

'It was going to take us five years to pay for the bakery, so we weren't allowed to spend a cent,' Gail adds. 'Well, three years in, shock-horror: I fell pregnant.'

They've come a long way from the early days, when they arrived with barely a thing, and slept in the room out the back for 13 years before moving to a property just outside town. They've raised four children there, and now are helping to raise their seven grandchildren.

'We arrived with a Datsun, two bean bags and a Hitachi TV,' Kevin laughs. 'And that was it. They left us with a double bed, so that was great.'

The original shop which houses the bakery was opened in 1890. It became a bakery in 1928 and celebrated its ninetieth year as a continuous bakery in 2018.

It's still very much a family affair, with two of Kevin and Gail's four children involved – Brad is a baker and Carly decorates the cakes. On competition day, it's all hands on deck. The boys – Brad and Nick – come in at around 2am.

'Sometimes we get caught with the footy and it's very busy with all the pies and all the rolls for football,' Kevin says.

Kevin won't work that day, but comes in fresh at 6.30am as the boys are finishing off.

'I just get set up, get everything ready, and the three of us do basically what we do, then we work together,' he says. 'We put it in the cool room, I go home and have a shower, I come back and cut out the best ten, naturally the best six for the judges.'

He doesn't just live vanilla slice – he dreams it too. He credits his recent successes to an epiphany he had in the middle of the night about how to improve his custard recipe.

'The funny thing was we won it in 2009 and we never went near it in '10 and '11, and I was missing something,' he explains. 'I woke up at one in the morning and I woke Gail and I said, I've got it! We will win it. We will never get beat again. She said, oh yeah, right, and we won three of the next five.'

He won't reveal the secret. Not even to *Back Roads*.

So intense is the contest that other bakeries will buy their competitors' vanilla slices to dissect and study to improve their own recipes. Kevin knows, because he does it too. One year a friend picked up six slices for him from a bakery 340 kilometres away.

'You know the bakeries to check out,' he says. 'The pastry, the thickness, how much they bake it, what they do with it. Their icing, flavour in the custard. All that sort of stuff.'

Kevin loves learning something new about vanilla slices, even today, as he strives for perfection. It's probably why he gets so upset when he hears the affectionate schoolyard name for the pastry: 'snot blocks'.

'Isn't that a terrible name? I hate it,' Kevin shudders. 'I don't even like hearing it.'

Crafting the slice is a three-person job. Out the back in the bakery's engine room are Kevin, his son Brad – an employee of 22 years – and Nick, known by the others as Bob, who started as an intern 14 years ago.

It's a large room, with white walls and stainless steel benches. In a corner dozens of loaves of bread are cooling on a tall silver trolley. Right now, they're preparing the custard. Kevin stands in front of a massive silver bowl, wielding a giant whisk. The cream has been whipped for nine minutes.

'One of the most important things is that you want a beautiful creamy custard,' says Kevin, whacking the whisk hard to free the excess cream.

'That's beautiful, look at it.'

Kevin is dressed in black uniform and apron clouded with patches of white flour. They match the streaks in his brown hair. He's preparing two large trays, which will make 100 vanilla slices in total.

'The real key to them is that they are fresh,' he insists.

They keep making trays of vanilla slice throughout the day as demand requires. It takes about an hour to make a new batch.

'We've got bakeries that do up to six trays and that will do them for two or three days. Bloody awful.' He shakes his head. 'We can make it at one o'clock in the afternoon. It all depends. You might have half a dozen grey nomads rock up in their caravans and wipe you out.'

Brow furrowed in concentration, Kevin scoops out a giant gloop of creamy custard with his hands and works it onto the thin sheet of freshly baked pastry. When the custard is all spread evenly, the crisp top is carefully lowered on. Then the icing, white and shiny, is tipped out of a silver saucepan and guided into place with a wooden spoon.

Kevin then smooths it with a palette knife, sliding it back and forth over the top as if spreading thick paint, covering every corner.

'When we were filming the [Back Roads] show, I reckon I iced it the worst I've ever iced it,' he cringes at the memory.

The vanilla slice competition started in 1998 in Ouyen, about 90 minutes north of Birchip. The story goes that then Victorian Premier Jeff Kennett had proclaimed a vanilla slice there the best he'd ever tasted. The event steadily grew. And grew. In 2012, it moved to Merbein.

It's a three-hour drive for Kevin and Gail from their bakery on competition day. The slices are transported in plastic containers in a large blue cooler in the back of the van.

But things haven't gone smoothly this morning.

'The icing's not 100 per cent,' Kevin says, as he reaches in and gently lifts the containers from the back of the vehicle. 'We are never, ever quite happy, are we, but we'll see what the judges think.'

The atmosphere is tense as an official tries to locate their entry form.

'Now, have you got your plates yet?' An organiser hands Kevin a standard white plate with a paper doily.

Hand trembling slightly, Kevin uses a spatula to remove his exhibits one by one. Then they join the other entries for judging, all on an endless narrow table covered with a white paper tablecloth. Some slices have a swirled chocolate pattern; others are slightly taller. Or wider.

Chief Judge Jason Riley explains what they are looking for to *Back Roads* presenter Heather Ewart: 'We look for obviously a smooth custard, vanilla flavouring through the custard. From there, we look at the crisp, crunchy pastry – not overbaked, but nice and light – and crisp as well. And finished off with the fondant icing, making sure it's got a nice little sheen and it's got the ability to reset.

'And obviously then with the taste testing, we look for the overall balance just to make sure that every aspect complements each other. We are not trying to reinvent the wheel – we are just looking for a nice vanilla slice.'

But some people are trying to reinvent the wheel. The innovation category is a revelation. A whole new world of vanilla slice, offering flavours like peanut butter and fairy floss. There are green flower decorations and meringue toppings.

For Kevin, however, there is only one prize that matters. The professional class. Outside the tent the crowds are gathering on white plastic seats, waiting for the winner of Kevin's class to be announced.

'This is the moment we have all been waiting for – and it's the winner in class,' the MC on stage announces. He's standing next to someone in a spongy yellow vanilla slice costume. 'And the winner in class this year comes from ... the Golden Nugget Bakery in Ballarat.'

In defeat, Kevin and Gail are pragmatic. They won't be stopped. They'll be back next year.

'It's a tough competition – well done, Ballarat,' Kevin says. 'They ran second last year. They've been knocking on the door.'

Two years have passed since *Back Roads*' visit. It's now early 2018. Business in Birchip is still going strong. The 2015 failure was eclipsed by success in 2016.

'I was shattered we didn't win that year,' Kevin says, 'but we won it the next.'

But weighing more heavily on Kevin's mind is the future of the competition itself.

The Great Australian Vanilla Slice Triumph is huge and it takes a lot of organising. In Merbein, the population swells from less than 3000 to 10,000 on the day of the contest, and they would sell 16,000 vanilla slices in a single day.

After the 2016 win, though, it had become unexpectedly engulfed in controversy. The fatigued committee of volunteers in Merbein wanted to hand the event on to another small, but passionate, town to ensure its future success. They thought they had the ideal candidate in Birchip – as it's bakery's repeat winner Kevin had a link to their town, having grown up in Merbein. The committee approached him to see if Birchip would be interested. He took the idea back to Birchip and was told 'Go for it!'

'So then it was announced that the vanilla slice competition was coming to Birchip,' Kevin recalls. 'There was a real kerfuffle over it.'

43

The hiccup was that the nearby town of Ouyen – which had started the competition, and run it for 14 years before handing it on to Merbein – hadn't been consulted. And it certainly didn't want the event leaving the municipality. It made national headlines. Even today Kevin feels saddened by it all.

'I feel like they think I tried to steal it.'

Gail says Kevin even considered quitting the competition when the event restarted in Mildura in 2017.

'We went but didn't do any good at all,' Kevin adds.

Despite the disappointment, Kevin hasn't lost his passion for vanilla slices, or the contest. Or his bakery.

'I just love the job,' he enthuses. 'There are very few jobs in the bakery that I don't enjoy doing. Our last batch of bread comes out at nine in the morning, so the smell of the bread goes right over the town.'

Kevin and Gail don't plan on going anywhere.

'We had an opportunity to sell up and go,' Kevin reveals. 'Anyway, I told Gail at the kitchen table, and all the kids and Gail started crying. I said, right, I'll never bring that up again.'

They bought a caravan to go travelling in, but they say they miss their children and grandchildren too much to stay away too long.

'It's Birchip Cemetery for me,' Gail says.

Kevin adds, 'Well, because you're there, I'm there.'

4

Natimuk

Location: 324 km north-west of Melbourne.

Population: 514

Aired: *Back Roads* visited Natimuk in late 2017 to film for its fourth season, which aired in 2018.

CRAGGY MOUNT ARAPILES RISES sharply from the flat farming pastures of northern Victoria's Wimmera Plains like a beacon. Nothing for kilometres. As far as the eye can see. The massive rock formation towering over the symmetrical lines of wheat paddocks draws climbers from around Australia, and the world, like a magnet.

Louise Shepherd should know. She first fell under Mount Arapiles' spell in the late 1970s. Within five years she'd moved there permanently.

'I never really thought when I first moved that I would be here nearly 40 years later, but here I am,' she smiles. 'Arapiles is everything. It's my recreation. It's my work. It's like a little oasis or a castle. It's a private playground as well as my workplace. It's only ten minutes up the road, and it's far enough away from the big cities that it feels fairly isolated.'

After that first taste of Mount Arapiles, Louise would go on to become one of the world's most eminent female rock climbers. It's a world full of daring and adventure. And technical terms and jargon. It's a whole new language.

Photos in Louise's home in nearby Natimuk show her on the cover of magazines with titles like *Australian Wild* and *Rock*. In one photo she is clinging to the underside of a large crack in a jaw-dropping sheer rock face. It looks as if she's gripping on for dear life with her fingertips.

'Some people love climbing for the adventure; some people love climbing for the movement on rock; and then there's everything in between – shades of grey,' she explains.

For Louise, it's the adventure, the social aspect, the physical side of exercising an array of different muscles as much as the problem-solving.

'You are trying to work out how to get up this bit of rock using whatever technique you can,' she says. 'Peak experience for me is when I'm climbing something I haven't climbed before and I'm solving the problems of how to get up this little bit of rock in front of me; at the same time I'm scanning the entire climb to work out where the next rest is going to be, and kind of working out a pathway up. The biggest thrill is solving the problem without falling off.'

But there are new, more daunting, problems in Louise's life. 'This is cancer,' Louise shrugs, pointing to a white bandage around her right arm. 'I've got a sarcoma. I'm going to have an operation in about a week and a half. The plastic surgeon says I'll never climb again after the operation. Anyway, we'll see. I'm in denial about it, a bit.'

The words hang in the air.

Louise is taut and wiry from decades of pulling herself up sheer rock faces. She has a warm, melodic laugh and a ruddy face. But her voice is as stable and solid as the rocks she loves climbing. Barely a crack. Pragmatic. She could be reading from a shopping list.

It's resignation, Louise explains. Submitting to what will be. In some ways it's the opposite of climbing, where it's your skills and your analysis and your strength that will get you to the top.

But there's also trust involved in rock climbing. Trust in the equipment and the team. And Louise fully trusts her team of surgeons.

She first noticed the lump about 18 months ago. Smaller than a marble, beneath her skin. It was diagnosed as a lipoma – benign fatty tissue. And diagnosed again and again, even as it grew larger, to the golf ball size it is now.

'It's never hurt,' she says. 'It still doesn't hurt now. I mean, if I lie on it in bed I can still feel the pressure. It's actually more my elbow that's a little bit tender than the actual lump.'

Eventually, Louise mentioned to the doctor that she'd like to have it removed. He sent her to a surgeon, who diagnosed it as cancerous. That was about six weeks ago. In ten days' time she will undergo the operation to have it removed. But it could come at a terrible price.

'Unfortunately for me, the sarcoma is pressing up against my triceps,' she says. 'And the surgeon who does the removal has to chop out my triceps, has to remove my triceps to secure the cancer, to make sure it's all gone. And unfortunately, the plastic surgeon says he's got to remove my latissimus, this muscle here' – she reaches behind her, partway down her back – 'this big back muscle, to repair the triceps.'

The latissimus dorsi, commonly known as the lat, is a large triangle-shaped muscle of the back and is used for doing things like pull-ups or swimming. It's essential for climbing.

'Now, you need a triceps for ordinary everyday life. You need it for rock climbing; you need it for everything. You cannot even put down a cup on the table without your triceps. But if you're an average person you don't need a latissimus. But if you're a rock climber you need your latissimus.'

Her voice wavers. Ever so slightly.

At the top of Mount Arapiles, the sun catches the lichen, turning dull grey boulders into freckled orange clumps.

Back in time, it is believed the Djuirite Balug and the Wotjobaluk, the traditional owners of this area, would scale the cliffs to chip off the hard quartzite sandstone for shaping into stone tools.

Later, in 1836, the Scottish explorer Major Thomas Mitchell would sentimentally name it after the Spanish hills near where the Battle of Salamanca took place during the Napoleonic Wars some 24 years earlier. But to the climbers who pilgrimage to its base from around Australia and the world, it's known simply as 'Araps' or 'the Piles'.

The first recreational climbers were drawn here in the 1960s. Later that decade, they'd already forged 230 climbing paths with names such as Tiptoe Ridge and Watchtower Crack. These days there are more than 3000 different climbs recorded and described in guidebooks.

Of course, there aren't too many climbs, especially on Arapiles, that Louise hasn't done before. She's a veteran of the climbing game, and an instructor, mentor and friend to many younger women who have come after her.

'It's a very, very good office. That's what I always think about when I'm halfway up a cliff, on a beautiful day.'

Some of the best days are captured in climbing books in Louise's modest home in Natimuk, about 12 kilometres from Mount Arapiles. Describing her as a role model for female climbers, the books note that her ascents of the North Wales climb Lord of the Flies and Derbyshire's London Wall 'astounded the British climbing scene'.

She's done thousands and thousands of climbs. And at least 60 new ascents – meaning she was the first one to climb and as such, had the privilege of naming the route and rating its difficulty in the climbing grading system (1–35) for the next guidebook.

Climb names might refer to an area – like the Organ Pipes, with individual climbs called D Major, D Minor, Didgeridoo and Horn Piece.

'But then some people leave their stamp on a climb by giving it a bizarre climb name,' Louise says. Names like

Deformed Port Salesman and Wub Direct. Louise named one of her first ascents Diazepam after the drug that calms the brain and the nerves.

'It's a bit of a joke. This climb is going to make you so hyper that you are going to need something to calm you down at the top,' she laughs.

Louise has just returned from a trip to Tasmania where she did two new ascents. She's named them My Brilliant Career and Live and Lat Be in reference to her uncertain climbing future.

Louise, humble and understated, is proudest of some of the climbs she did in the 1980s and 1990s, making her way up from the ground to the dizzy heights with no pre-knowledge, on the first attempt.

It was very much a male-dominated sport back then, although Louise says she did have incredible female role models before her. In 1981 when she became the first person to onsight climb Trojan at Mount Arapiles, a 25-grade climb she completed in one go without any prior knowledge, one of her male fellow climbers joked that they'd have to start taking her seriously now.

The sport has changed in many ways over time.

In her heyday, Louise's strength was her ability to climb from the bottom to the top in one go, without falling off. She says it's a mental, as well as physical discipline.

'Now I'm just kind of humbled by my own strength and I just completely took it for granted,' she says.

It's the ultimate risk analysis – pushing yourself and your equipment as far to the edge as possible.

'Some people, some of my friends, are incredibly strong, way stronger than me, but they fall off earlier than me, or they come down earlier because they haven't got the mental strength to hang in there and think, if I fall off here I'm not going to actually hurt myself; I'm just going to have a little two-metre fall on the rope and it's perfectly safe because it's overhanging; there's no ledges in the way; I'm perfectly fine,' Louise explains. 'And there are other people who would be able to solo that piece without a rope at all, because they are even stronger, mentally, than me. I'm probably somewhere in the middle of the road.'

Climbing has left an indelible mark on the traditional farming community of nearby Natimuk. In the beginning, climbers would gather and live semi-permanently in tents in the camp area called the Pines, named for the trees planted to commemorate the centenary of Major Mitchell's visit. It was pretty basic: there were toilets, but no showers. Every so often the climbers would take a day off and travel the 34 kilometres into Horsham for a shower and some shopping.

They were a colourful and bohemian bunch. They loved the environment, and wanted to minimise their impact on the planet. They lived frugally. One couple had a massive tent they'd received as a wedding present, which they called the Taj Mahal. They would only go into Natimuk to buy milkshakes. Or to the post office to pick up their unemployment cheques.

Louise first got a glimpse of the community she would join when she came for a long weekend in 1978.

'It was just like this whole new world. It was like a revelation,' she says.

It was a freewheeling life. People would climb during the spring, summer and autumn, and then head up to Queensland for the winter, to climb at a cliff called Frog Buttress, near Boonah, south-west of Brisbane. Then they might do some work, then go travelling overseas.

The full-time climbers were called 'dirtbags'. The farmers called them 'the goats'.

'People would come and go a bit,' Louise recalls. 'There were a lot of colourful characters back then who had, you know, pretty bizarre haircuts and clothing.'

Yet for all the carefree camping way of life, they were serious about their climbing.

'There was, you know, a lot of intense rivalry between a few climbers, and everyone was doing new routes too,' Louise says. 'Everyone was scoping out new climbs but being very secretive about it because you didn't want anyone to steal your new route. So people would go sneaking off early in the morning and they'd go and, you know, scope out their new climb: abseil down it and make sure there was enough protection on it to be able to come back and do it.'

Casual or part-time work supplemented the climbing lifestyle.

'A lot of us did grape picking up at Mildura in the Riverland during the summer period and then that money would last; you could make it last for months and months because back then there was no fee for camping at Arapiles,' she says. 'For a year or two it was very easy to live very cheaply and very frugally.'

Slowly, the climbers moved out of their tents and into town. They'd buy up the old houses at bargain prices, raise families, and unfurl their creativity on the town. Over time, there was recognition that the climbers were bringing new life to the community.

'Natimuk is still a traditional farming community,' Louise says. 'Nowadays, it's recognised that climbers add a lot to the local economy and climbers are completely integrated – or more or less completely integrated – now. They used to do weird things like they'd play chess in the pub. That was a big no-no back in the day because locals found that very confronting.'

The climbers started a biennial arts festival, the Nati Frinj Biennale, in 2000. It's a relaxed, innovative and quirky festival which draws a wide audience, both of locals and travellers from Melbourne and beyond. Climbers also continue to travel from around the world to the big rock.

'A lot of little country towns are dying because the young people are moving away to the cities for work or for study, and some of them are coming back, but a lot of them aren't,' Louise points out. 'But Natimuk is sort of bucking the trend – a lot of young people are leaving but they're coming back, moving back. Other people are moving into town.'

Arapiles is unique as a climbing area because it's got good climbing at all grades, from beginners to hard climbs.

Louise took up climbing after her boyfriend at the time suggested they try this new sport. She was 20 years old.

'He said why don't we give it a go? And we had no clue,' Louise says. 'We went to the Grampians [in Victoria] and, on the way, we bought a marine rope. You know, one of those plastic ropes. You put a match to it, it melts. It smokes and melts into this blob of black. You know – it's not a climbing rope at all! Well we didn't know that, we had no clue. It was cheap. Afterwards we used it as a washing line.'

They walked up an easy slab called The Elephant's Hide, near Halls Gap. She remembers wrapping the rope around the boulder and lowering her body, hand over hand, down a steep section. Burning.

'It was completely stupid and pointless,' she says.

But it was a start. And enough to enliven a feeling in Louise that she's never been able to shrug off.

They saw some 'proper' rock climbers on the same trip.

'We realised that what we were doing was nothing like rock climbing was supposed to be,' Louise says.

Back in 1978, there wasn't a single climbing shop in Adelaide, where they lived. The couple met a man selling climbing gear to a local club out of his garage in the suburbs. He offered to show them how to use the equipment.

'It was very addictive ... once we realised how it should be done,' she reflects.

They got to know some other climbers, who invited them for a long weekend at Mount Arapiles. And it's fair to say Louise's life hasn't been the same since.

She went travelling and rock climbing overseas, and camped at the Pines in between, until her then boyfriend bought an old house at Natimuk. Louise eventually bought him out and lived there for 30 years, welcoming climbers from around Australia and the world.

Louise started a rock climbing company in 1988 to teach others, but eventually sold out of it. She's still employed as a guide, taking groups up Arapiles, including beginners and even schoolchildren. She notes that people who might not be great at traditional sports can still do rock climbing.

'A lot of climbing is actually in the head more than the body,' she reckons.

You do need a sense of adventure and a desire to challenge yourself. 'What I like to do is find a climb that's going to be challenging enough but not so hard that I have no hope of getting up it.'

While she's experienced, Louise says she isn't as strong as she used to be. She thinks she reached her climbing peak in her twenties and thirties. She's never hurt herself badly rock climbing, though she's fallen many times. She still remembers her first fall. Vividly.

'I broke a rock off on a climb – not Arapiles, another climbing area in the Flinders Rangers, which is a lot looser,' she recalls. 'I probably went about ten metres. I had one piece of protection which held – thank goodness.

'It profoundly shocked me. It was my first leader fall ever. I wasn't expecting it. I got to the top of the cliff and burst into tears and my male climbing partners didn't know what to do because nobody cried back then.'

She didn't hurt herself, but she became 'obsessive' about testing the rock first, and making sure she places plenty of protection devices into the rock to break her fall.

'Trust is a big part of rock climbing. You've got to trust yourself. More than that, you've got to trust the other person holding the rope. You've got to really trust them. So a lot of accidents happen when two people climbing don't know each other.'

Louise's lounge room walls are lined with photos of her climbing mates in action.

'Somebody said [to me] you'll be able to do slab climbs,' Louise says, referring to the easiest level of ascent. After she has her lump removed, they meant.

'Well, as it happens, I hate slab climbs. I was like, oh, that's so boring! Look, we're just going to wait and see. They may not take the whole lat.'

She's told the surgeons she's a rock climber and a guide, and even posted photos to them, showing herself scaling enormous cliff faces. Just to remind them to save her muscles if they can.

'I'm sort of trying not to think too much about it and try and take it one day at a time,' she says.

Postscript: Louise was in hospital for ten days. The orthopedic surgeon removed a small amount of one of her triceps, and not the entire muscle. This meant her latissimus dorsi did not have to be used in the procedure. Louise's medical team is confident she will be able to climb again.

5

Harrow

Location: 363 km north-west of Melbourne.

Population: 200

Aired: The *Back Roads* crew filmed in Harrow during the second series in 2016. A week before the episode aired, one of the much-loved members of the community who would appear in the show, Tari Sondhu, took his own life.

GURJIT SONDHU IS CLAPPING loudly and banging against the side of her white utility: 'Hey! Come on! *Move* it!'

She accelerates gently forward towards the mob of wayward sheep. There's at least 70 standing there, staring at the vehicle. Some don't even bother to look up from the forbidden grain they are busy munching off the dirt.

Gurjit blasts the horn. She's at home behind the wheel of the dusty ute, even in her stylish checked trousers and linen charcoal top. She's wearing dark sunglasses, pretty red lipstick, and an air of calm.

It takes a few encouraging honks and collectively, the sheep soon get the message, gazing at her curiously, before, as one, they slowly turn and trot off towards the paddock.

It's an overcast day and thick white cloud hangs low in the sky, just above the gum trees lining the fence. The sheep had slipped out through an open gate to greedily snack at the grain stores, close to the house.

Gurjit loves it here. She's been in Harrow 42 years now. And despite the tragedy and heartbreak she's suffered here, she wouldn't want to be anywhere else. She even loves her misbehaving sheep, and the Black Angus beef cattle which roam around the 2023-hectare property called Jullundur.

It's been more than a year since the horrific day when her husband of 40 years took his own life after his mental illness spiralled out of control. The pain was immense. It reverberated around the close-knit community of Harrow.

It's a beautiful town, in every way. From the majestic red gums that frame the Glenelg River at the entrance to town, to how the community pulled together for working bees and a memorial service after Tari's death.

One day follows. And then another. And you find your way, Gurjit says: 'The sheep still needed feeding. Actually, work was the only thing keeping me going. So I put myself into feeding the sheep. I didn't even think about Tari or anybody else. I thought about the farm.

'I had a choice – what do I do now, look after this farm

or sit down and just be stressed? And I've just put myself into the work.'

Harrow, one of Victoria's oldest inland settlements, has had its own struggles over the years since it was officially proclaimed in the 1840s. Despite the rich farming country, it's been hit at times by drought and flooding. But it always bounces back.

Decades ago the town held an event called Beaut Blokes, highlighting their single male residents, in an attempt to draw new women to the town as numbers dwindled.

Gurjit came to Harrow via a different path, from India in the 1970s. Which makes her decision to stay and run the property herself, with love, all the more extraordinary. Gurjit was just 17 when she moved to Harrow from the town of Mullanpur in Punjab in 1976. Her parents had arranged the marriage to a man she barely knew. Her knowledge of the massive continent was sparse: it had sheep and cows, and was a dry place – basic information she'd picked up in geography class long before there was any inkling of the significance the country would come to have in her life.

'That's the only thing I knew about Australia, nothing else,' she says.

She had a big family in India – 30 cousin-sisters. There were many family get-togethers, full of laughter, shrieking and bright silks. At her own home, she grew up with servants around her tending to the cooking, cleaning and washing.

She was sitting for her year 12 exams when her parents told her a young man was visiting from Australia to look for a wife. He was a relative of one of her sisters' husbands and he was meeting with several families. His name was Avtar Sondhu. Tari for short.

'I wasn't even in the picture I was too young. I was only 17,' Gurjit recalls.

She came home from school one day and the Sondhu family was there.

'I saw this young man and never really took much notice, as he was about 26 – all I remember is that he was wearing a purple suit,' she says. 'Tari was proud of his pure merino purple woollen suit purchased from Myers. It was the '70s.'

She heard a few days later that the family had liked her, and then things happened pretty quickly. She was married within a few weeks. All before she'd had time to digest what it would mean.

'My father asked me but I was very naïve,' Gurjit says. 'If I had to do it again probably I would say no because I was only 17; I'd never seen life and what life is all about. But when you are 17 it's yes, getting married, and the jewellery and the clothes and the saris, and it all comes with the wedding. A 17-year-old girl, she's not thinking about settling in Australia and what she's going to do for work. I was more thinking about the pretty clothes I would have.

When I got married I thought it would be very romantic living on a farm as in the Bollywood movies, dancing and singing in the fields. I thought, oh wow, I'm marrying an Australian farmer – and my family said they have a big farm and I thought, they have a big farm: they would have servants, you know? I don't have to do anything, I just have to live the life of luxury. What a dream!'

It took a few months for the visa to Australia to come through, and suddenly Gurjit's life took a dramatic turn.

'It was pretty hard for me. I didn't have any idea about Tari, and Tari didn't have any idea about me,' she says. 'I thought marriage was something, you know, you just live happily ever after. Actually, in real life, things don't work like that.'

The new couple flew into Melbourne from New Delhi in July 1976. It was bitterly cold and raining when they pulled up into the 4000-acre (1600-hectare) farm, Mullagh Station, in Harrow, four hours west of Melbourne.

'I remember I had a red sari on. I was dressed up like a bride,' Gurjit says. 'With all the trimmings. The next morning when I got up, I had no idea what I was getting myself into. Tari got up and he started dressing up in his farming clothes. In India he was dressing better. I'm looking at him, he had the patchy trousers on; you know, farmers wear the patchy trousers. I thought, they have a few dollars, why are they wearing that? I had no idea what he was up to. He was going to go crutch the sheep.'

She continued dressing up in her bright saris for a few weeks, until she realised nobody was taking notice of her beautiful clothes. Everybody was too consumed in their own work. Even today, she remembers the desperate anxiety of homesickness. The tight, raw knot deep inside her. In a new country, with only basic English. Away from her big, noisy family.

'I had a different view of coming to Australia,' she says. 'I probably thought I was going to get pampered by the family; there was going to be a big deal made about me, the bride coming in this and that. It was nothing like that. In India it is: when the new bride comes the family make a big fuss, but here nobody did anything. They were just typical Aussie farmers. They were more worried about the shearing coming up. We have to crutch the sheep, they are getting too daggy, you know. Rather than worry about this girl coming from India.'

Tari's family came to Harrow from India back in the 1890s. Tari's great-uncle Indar Singh Sondhu had paved the way for the family. He was a businessman who had started with nothing and became an Indian hawker in the region. He bought into general stores, and eventually Mullagh Station in 1939. Twenty years later, as he got too old to run the property alone, he sent for his two nephews in India – Tari's father, Swaran Singh Sondhu, and brother, Dharam Singh Sondhu. They left their families in India to make a new life in Harrow and became valued members of the community.

Australia's immigration was still governed by the White Australia policy, and the visas for the men's families in India took years. Tari was seven years old when he moved to Australia. The separation from his father had a big impact on him.

By the time Gurjit arrived 20 years later, immigration was easier. But life was still hard. A few weeks after she arrived, Tari's mother suggested Gurjit take lunch to the boys in the shearing shed. They were crutching – removing the clumps of manure-laden wool, called dags, from around the rear legs and tails of the sheep. Gurjit was still dressing up around the farm.

'I walked into the shed and Tari said, "Pick the dag up,"' she says. 'Just straight away, never thinking this girl would have no idea what a dag is, he said, "Clean it. Get the broom and clean it." 'I looked at him I said "Oh my God." He meant to tell me pick this up. It's disgusting. How could he do that? I had the nail polish on and my hand was pretty nice, and I was absolutely disgusted.'

Tari insisted – despite Gurjit's tears – and she used a tea towel from the food basket to cover the clump and remove it.

'That was my introduction to picking the dags up,' she says. 'Now I don't even think about it. Dags are worth money.'

Isolated and feeling alone, Gurjit started practising English with Tari's little brother, David, to expand her vocabulary. Until then she'd been speaking in Hindi and Punjabi.

'I could understand English but to speak it was very difficult – I had an accent and was shy too,' she says. 'I would sit in the room and cry. It's a pretty lonely place here. I'd come from India, a big family, and always in the family you've always got something happening: weddings and birthdays, some sort of celebration. But here it's nothing.'

The only connection to the community was the weekly football matches to watch Tari play for the B side. She would dress up in her sari and the whole family would go. She couldn't understand the rules of the game but enjoyed the atmosphere. And the view.

'I couldn't understand but they had pretty damn good bodies,' she laughs. 'I was more or less looking at them, how good-looking they were.'

The couple had their first son, Jason, a couple of years after Gurjit arrived. Two more children, Belinda and Philip, followed, and slowly Gurjit got to know other young mothers at the school, who became her friends. Even so, it took her a good 15 years to shake off the homesick feeling for her old life in India.

These days, Harrow is home.

'It took me a long time but now I just feel this is home. This is a real home and this is our children's home and grandchildren; this is their home too,' she says.

One of the first projects Gurjit embarked on when she stepped up to run the farm recently was to landscape a garden around the house. And to fix the fences on the property. A row of blooming white rose bushes now greets visitors at the entrance, and a grand circular pond is awaiting completion. It's both beautiful and tranquil. The day promises rain, and Gurjit is hopeful her pond may be filled.

Out the back, fruit trees are dotted through plump, inviting grass. A green swing set sits expectantly. Gurjit has five grandchildren, who visit regularly from Melbourne.

'We are slowly getting there,' Gurjit says. 'My garden is getting a little bit better than what it was. When you are working hard you want to come home to a nice place. My husband used to say, if you live in the house you just want to sit here. I just want it to feel like a resort.'

The couple built the new house on the property four years ago and had planned to retire in the house there, and eventually let their children, and grandchildren, take over the running of the farm.

'We had a bit of a family meeting before we built the house; what are we going to do?' she says. 'The boys said they loved the farm. All three children, they loved the farm – there is so much connection to the farm.'

Tari and Gurjit moved out of the Sondhu family partnership and started farming on their own in 1989. It was the year the wool price crashed and quite a tough year. But slowly they managed to get through it.

'My husband was a very good businessman and he used to say if you don't have the money, don't spend it,' Gurjit says.

She is full of kind words about Tari, who was heavily involved in the community, and a generous husband and father.

But Tari had unresolved issues with his own father. He thought he had time to make peace but his father died before this could happen. Gurjit says Tari couldn't let go of the past and by early 2016 his behaviour had grown erratic. Gurjit didn't know the warning signs, but she can recognise them now.

'Life is not meant to be easy. Every marriage you've got problems – nothing is smooth sailing,' she says. 'I was finding he was getting very short-tempered. It was very hard on me because every time something went wrong on the farm I got the blame. I'm not the argumentative type. I just tried to keep things calm but he would always find a fault.'

He never showed that side of himself to the public, but at home he would grow upset at minor things. Gurjit says she didn't realise it was depression, but in hindsight it seemed obvious.

'I did say to him a few times, something's not right, the way you behave sometimes,' Gurjit says. 'I said, when you are good you are really good; when you get into these moods it's not normal.'

When *Back Roads* came and filmed in September and October 2016, Tari was his 'normal' self. 'He was fine, he was really good. He was very excited,' Gurjit recalls.

Tari was a generous host, full of humour and stories, and revelling in having his family around him. During the interview with host Heather Ewart, Tari and Gurjit laughed as they shared funny stories from farm life. But by January 2017 his depression had taken hold. Gurjit had gone with him to the doctor just before Christmas and told the physician she was worried about Tari. But then he passed a mental health assessment with flying colours.

'He was a very intelligent man. He'd never want to be beaten,' she says.

He was proud, and tried to hide his illness in public. But that Christmas, Gurjit says, he was spaced out, and he would spend hours lying in bed. This was unusual.

'I think he was feeling very, very anxious,' Gurjit says. 'I didn't realise that was depression, and then his temperament just got worse and worse and I just could not cope. He wasn't happy. I couldn't do anything right in the end. I could not do anything right.'

Gurjit found she couldn't go anywhere in the house without Tari growing anxious about where she'd gone. She was growing exhausted.

'Mentally, I was just getting really stressed out. I didn't know what to do,' she says.

She confided in a few friends. He was becoming more and more difficult. It was like she was walking on eggshells, waiting for him to explode. His speech became confused. One minute he'd be telling family or friends about a holiday he wanted to take. The next he was worried about the farm.

'I was scared because I didn't want to get up in the morning and wonder what sort of mood he would be in,' she says. 'I wouldn't tell anybody. I kept a lot inside. I needed help but I didn't know which way to go. Tari was such a proud man. He reckoned he had a good name in the community. He didn't want anybody to know what was going on.'

It's hard to ask for help.

'When he was happy he was a completely different person. He couldn't do enough for you,' she says. 'In public we were like a perfect couple but when we came home I was always at fault.'

Gurjit felt as if she was dying inside. Then the day before he died, he'd woken up so angry. She'd never seen him like that before.

'He wasn't himself. Now I'm realising it wasn't my fault or his fault, it was the depression. It's a disease. It's happened to a lot of people out there.'

The next day Gurjit rose early to go to her regular exercise class in Harrow, a 15-minute drive away.

When she came home just after 7am her husband was in her face. She didn't feel safe so she left immediately. She drove to a friend's place and contacted her children. The police rang the family a short time later to tell them Tari was dead.

'He was a good man; he was a really good man, but he had a problem. He had a really bad problem. Nobody could solve it.'

Looking back, Gurjit says she'd try and get him hospitalised by force, if necessary, though it's hard to see a solution when you are in the middle of the crisis.

Tari was a much-loved member of the Harrow community, Gurjit says, and she was so grateful for the way the community banded together to organise the memorial and make sure she had help on the farm. A week after Tari died, the community gathered in the pub for drinks for Tari, and the screening of the *Back Roads* episode about the town. The family wanted the program to go ahead, as a reminder of much happier times, rather than pull the episode.

'He was loved by everybody. He loved the community. That was his good side,' Gurjit says.

Fourteen months has passed since that terrible day. She is still replaying it in her mind.

'I'm still angry. I haven't forgiven him for what the family has suffered, but I am sorry for his mental suffering and not being able to help him.'

Gurjit has just returned from her first trip to India in 18 years to visit her family. It was part of her healing process.

'I was telling a friend this morning. I said I've been away for nearly six weeks. I haven't filled up a glass of water, or made a cup of tea. Or washed my clothes. Or cooked.'

It was a life she could have had, had she stayed in India all those years ago. But now Australia is home.

She wanted to go back to India reconnect with family, and find herself again.

'After being a wife, mother and grandmother for 40 years and putting my family first for those years, I had forgotten about my roots. I went back to my family home in India and I connected with my past.

'It was a peaceful calming of my mind and soul, but after weeks I started missing my family and home. It is refreshing to be back home at Jullundur. It is good to be back and part of this wonderful community. Jason, Belinda and Philip and their families enjoy coming to Jullundur frequently to catch up and lend a hand on the farm.

'Going back to India, I've found out about myself, which family I come from, why I behave the way I do.'

She wants to focus on the farm now. On the wayward sheep and the cattle.

'I said to the kids, now I'm back, this year is all about farming,' Gurjit says. 'I've got all the nonsense out of my head. My mind is cleaned. I'm focused and this is what I want to do from now on.

'I just feel peace. I feel peace in myself. Life is about forgiveness, love and peace.'

Note: If this story has raised issues for you or a loved one, please reach out for help.

Lifeline 13 11 14; www.lifeline.org.au
Suicide Call Back Service 1300 659 467;
www.suicidecallbackservice.org.au
MensLine Australia 1300 78 99 78;
www.mensline.org.au

6

Harrow's cricketers

What: Australia's first international sporting tour was by an Aboriginal cricket team from the Western District of Victoria. Their story is celebrated at the Harrow Discovery Centre and Johnny Mullagh Interpretive Centre. The team was officially recognised for the first time in 2002, when its contribution to the nation's sporting history was acknowledged in the Australian Sports Hall of Fame.

When: The team toured Victoria and New South Wales in 1866 and 1867, before travelling to England for a year. Tom Wills captained the side until early 1867, when English player Charles Lawrence took the helm.

Who: The first Australian XI consisted of Ngurrinmin/ Unaarrimin (Johnny Mullagh), Baldyanguk/Bullchanach (Harry Bullocky), Bunbarrngit/Bonnibarngeet (Tiger), Brim Bunya (Tommy Red Cap), Grougarrong (Mosquito, or James Cuzens), Yellanach (Johnny Cuzens), Yangendyinanyuk/

Jumgumjenanuke (Dick-a-Dick), Murrumgunarrimin/
Jarrawuk (Two Penny), Dyalaty Murrimin (Jim Crow),
Murrumgunerrimin (Jimmy Tarpot), Ngarramunidyarrimin
(Peter), Balarrimin Nyarringin (Sundown), Mijarrle
(Lake Billy), Cungewarrimim (Billy Officer), Hingingairah
(Harry Rose), Brapirr/Bripumyarrimin (King Cole),
Bripumgunarriman (Charley Dumas). Captain: Charles
Lawrence.

Three players reportedly died in 1867, the year before
the team set sail for England – Ngunarrimin/Unamurrimin
(Jelicoe), Pappinjurumun (Paddy) and Bilayarrimin (Watty).
NB There are many different spellings of the names. Where
possible and relevant, the spelling is based on the sound
system of the Wotjobaluk, who speak the Wergaia language.

THE 11 MEN ARE gazing patiently at the camera. Looking
serious. And slightly uncomfortable. The team of Aboriginal
cricketers is posing with their coach, holding the position
carefully for the large plate camera. One ... two ... three ...
flash.

It was the height of summer and any other week they
would have been sweltering, wearing constricting three-piece
woollen suits, with cravats tight around their necks, or the
odd bow tie. But fortunately, this week, in February 1867, it
was unseasonably cool.

They'd already played a run of cricket matches when
the photo beside the Members' Pavilion at the Melbourne
Cricket Ground was taken in early 1867. But there's no way

they could have foreseen the legacy they would leave. It was the start of a remarkable chapter in Australia's sporting and social history.

The photograph was taken before the team took to the field for a return match. Just six weeks earlier they'd taken to the same field for a match that had been lauded as one of the most significant ever played.

Some 8000 spectators had been drawn to the Melbourne Cricket Ground for the game between the Melbourne Cricket Club and the Aboriginal XI over two days, beginning on Boxing Day in 1866. The MCC team won quickly, so a scratch match was held over the remaining two days, in which the 'Natives' – made up of the best Aboriginal and white Australian-born cricketers playing together on one side – took on 'The World' – a team of immigrants. It remains a proud part of the MCG's history.

Many in the Aboriginal XI team would go on to tour England 13 months later, in Australia's first international sporting tour, long before the Ashes rivalry officially kicked off.

Standing in the second row of the photo is Ngurrinmin (Unaarrimin) from the Jardwadjali group in the Western District of Victoria. He was better known as Johnny Mullagh, after the station where he worked as a shearer. The star all-rounder would go on to gain a reputation as one of the most skilled cricketers of his time.

Today, 150 years later, the photograph has pride of place on the wall near the entrance of the Harrow Discovery Centre and Johnny Mullagh Interpretive Centre, an entire museum dedicated to these men from the Jardwadjali, Kirrae Whurrong, Gunditjmara, Mardityali and Wotjobaluk communities, in the main street of Harrow in Victoria's west Wimmera region, halfway between Adelaide and Melbourne.

Johnny Mullagh's name is ubiquitous in Harrow. It's everywhere in the museum. On the oval. Even at the local caravan park. And at Harrow Cemetery, where the star bowler and batsman was buried 125 years ago with his cricket bat and a set of stumps tied together in the local club's colours.

There's even a plaque set into rock on the ground where he hit a cricket ball across the main road, 138 metres from the crease.

Here Marks The Spot
Harrow's Longest Recorded Hit
JOHNNY MULLAGH
– UNAARRIMIN –
1878

Every year for the past two decades local and Indigenous players hold the Johnny Mullagh Cup, and other events, to celebrate an extraordinary man, team and story.

Josie Sangster has been working in the centre for the past seven months. She describes herself as a 'half-local', having lived in Harrow a decade, before moving away, and back again. She is still uncovering new pieces of information about the team, little nuggets that she files into the deep recesses of her brain to freely draw upon for the many tourists who pop into the museum.

'Most people when they come in, they say I know the story, but we'll just have a look and then you learn more, and more, and that leads you to further research, and you fall in love with the story,' she says.

The story starts on the large sheep stations surrounding Harrow in the 1850s. The gold rush around Ballarat, 250 kilometres to the east of Harrow, had drawn away numerous workers and many of their places were filled by Aboriginal men and women. They worked hard. It's unlikely they were all paid for their time, though some stations were said to be better than others.

In the downtime, they would play cricket.

'They would scratch out a pitch on their front paddock, put a few markers out and just have a game,' Josie says. 'They were encouraged to play, and everyone soon realised they were darn good.'

Ashley Couzens, a direct descendant of Grougarrong, or James Cuzens (whose brother was the bowler Yellanach, or Johnny Cuzens), believes the men would have just picked up the game by watching it and visualising movement and technique.

'To this day our kids are born into our way – we are visual learners,' he says. 'It's instilled from birth. This is passed down through generations and it's a key and important cultural part of our ongoing learning.'

Descendants today still share Yellanach's strong love of sport, as well as some of his other traits, such as his speed, skill and determination.

Cricket had become increasingly popular on western

Victorian sheep stations – backed by their sports-loving owners. More and more informal games were arranged.

Richard Kennedy is a descendant of Yangendyinanyuk, a stockman, all-round cricket player and impressive athlete, also known as Dick-a-Dick. He too grew up on stories of his great-great-grandfather, passed down to him through his grandfather, father and uncle.

'I've always known one of the members of the team was a relative,' Richard says. 'There's huge pride because they were a great cricket team. They only started learning the game a short time before they went overseas and they were playing against English players, where it was their traditional game.'

The first game by an all-Aboriginal side was held in the western Victorian town of Edenhope, in the dirt beside the woolshed at Bringalbert Station in January 1866. The Aboriginal side won easily. Some of the men were encouraged to join the local cricket team.

A group of station owners, including William Hayman from Lake Wallace Station, were involved in the club, and saw an opportunity to tour. The Melbourne Cricket Club agreed to a Boxing Day match. A well-known cricketer, Tom Wills, was dispatched to start training the all-Aboriginal side, and then travelled with the team to Melbourne for their first game at the MCG at the end of the year.

It wasn't just the spectacle of the game, mind you. After the cricket, the sportsmen would entertain the crowd with displays of their athletic prowess. For a price, spectators could compete against them. It helped fund the tour.

'They'd play the cricket and then perform the tricks and the sports afterwards, which was just as much of a drawcard,' Josie says.

A newspaper advertisement lists the competitions, tinged with the language of the time: 'Throwing boomerangs and spears by the whole of the natives'; a 100-yard and 440-yard flat race; standing high jump; a 100-yard race backwards. 'Throwing cricket ball': for a shilling, entrants could throw a ball at members of the team.

Yangendyinanyuk, or Dick-a-Dick, one of the most jovial and skilled athletes in the team, was particularly proficient at deflecting dozens of incoming cricket balls with a narrow wooden shield.

'He would be there with his shields and he'd just go bang, bang, bang, bang and no one ever got him. He was just too quick and his reflexes were fantastic,' Josie says.

He was also an outstanding performer in other events, and often won many of the contests. He consistently threw a cricket ball more than 100 yards (91 metres), and once as much as 113 yards (103 metres).

'Tribal displays' were another feature of the tour. The men would dress in costumes made from culturally significant possum skin, and lyrebird feathers. They would stage a mock battle, complete with long spears and war cries.

Descendant Ashley Couzens says he feels great pride at the inspiring story of the tour, tinged with sadness as one of the players, Brapirr (Bripumyarrimin), or King Cole, had died in London after contracting pneumonia while on the tour.

'My heart bleeds for the descendants of King Cole, who never got the opportunity to pass on his own country's cultural way with proper ceremony,' he says. 'The language used back then to describe us shows how far we have come in understanding our culture and sporting abilities and to be recognised as equal contributors and gatekeepers of this country.

'They were put on show as some sort of native novelty act with the crowds they drew and the tricks they did, but the other side of that is that it also opened up our culture to the world and showed our unique skills and abilities that exceeded that of the white man at the time,' he continues. 'And that sheer determination to survive how Australia was at the time when treated like second-class citizens.'

It was a different time and Australia was a different place. Racism was overt. The newspapers regularly referred to the Aboriginal cricketers as 'natives', 'blacks' or 'darkies'. Australia was yet to become a nation, and was still a series of colonies, each with its own laws and attitudes.

And there was tension between white settlers and the first Australians. In other parts of the country, there were violent clashes and many deaths. Just five years earlier, Tom Wills, the coach of the Aboriginal team, had come home to the remote central Queensland property his father had been settling to find him murdered, along with 18 others. It was the largest massacre of white settlers at the time, and led to bloody and indiscriminate retribution, which would kill tens of thousands of Aboriginal people.

In western Victoria, just a decade or two earlier, communities of Aborigines had been decimated in conflicts as the white settlers moved in. But on these stations in western Victoria, by the mid-1860s there appeared to be an amiable relationship between the Europeans and Indigenous workers.

As underdogs, the Aboriginal team playing at the MCG on those two days in December 1866 was well supported by the huge crowd, and their skill was admired.

It was at that Boxing Day match that the first seeds of an idea to tour England began to germinate. The English side had toured Australia for the first time five years earlier.

In the crowd at the Boxing Day match was a Sydney businessman and member of the Sydney cricket club known as the Albert Cricket Club. According to Rex Harcourt and John Mulvaney's comprehensive account of the tour, *Cricket Walkabout: The Aboriginal Cricketers of the 1860s*, the financier known as William Gurnett signed up the team and first proposed a tour to Sydney and England.

The details of the game, and the subsequent tour, are contained in a tall, black leather-bound volume at the Harrow Discovery Centre. 'Aboriginal Cricketers Scoring Book' is printed in gold on the cover.

After the game at the MCG, the team toured Victoria, travelling first by horse and cart to Geelong and then back to Collingwood, according to the scorebook. Then to Bendigo, Ballarat and back to Melbourne in early 1867 for a return match at the Melbourne Cricket Ground, where the famous black-and-white photo was taken. En route, some of the players contracted measles, and the tour hit some financial road bumps. In Sydney, the team played its first game at the

Albert Club's inner-city ground on 21–22 February, two months after their first game in Melbourne.

The deal fell apart. Cheques had been dishonoured. The tour to England fell over. The details are murky, although it is widely speculated that Gurnett was embezzling the funds.

The team forged through, though, with several members ill, under the guidance of an English cricketer, Charles Lawrence. Charles put all the men up at his hotel in Sydney. Charles was also a successful cricketer and coach at the Albert Club.

This part of the story wasn't fully understood until the 1980s, when a young Melbourne man, Ian Friend, was digging through some old family boxes belonging to his father, after his death.

'I knew nothing; knew nothing about it,' he says.

There was an old cricket bat in one box. A Bible in another. A few pendants. And a diary, an antique fob watch, newspaper clippings, photos and handwritten notes penned by Charles when he was in his eighties.

'There were a few old family chests there,' Ian says. 'Not just the one box – there were other boxes of family letters from the 1850s going back to England.

'I was pretty young, probably 26 or 27, something like that. My father obviously passed pretty young so didn't really tell me much. I have no idea if he knew the story, but he had all the information so I presume he would have.'

The story was scattered between several boxes. Little bits of information that Ian slowly pieced together. 'I'm very interested in family papers. I love that type of thing,' Ian says. 'This story, it just knocked me out.'

He read the diary. Around the same time, his great aunt had given him a book on cricket. It was *Cricket Walkabout* – the first edition, published in 1967. He realised they both told the story of the same cricket team.

Soon after, Ian went to watch his beloved Melbourne AFL team play at the Melbourne Cricket Ground and on a whim popped into the club's library to see if it had any further information about his great-great grandfather's team.

By chance, he met Rex Harcourt, co-author of *Cricket Walkabout*. He was astonished when Ian revealed he was a descendant of Charles Lawrence. Rex was excited to see Charles Lawrence's diary of the tour. 'That was a really good connection and then it all flourished from there I suppose,' Ian says.

Charles Lawrence was a great cricketer in his own right. He'd starting playing the game as a boy in England and Ireland, before being selected for the first English team, which toured to Australia in 1861–62.

After the tour, Charles was asked to stay on in Sydney at the Albert Club, to help raise the standard of cricket in the colony. That's where his world, and the Aboriginal team's worlds, converged.

At Harrow Discovery Centre, Josie Sangster is flipping through the pages of the scorebook. Coach Tom Wills had been filling out the pages for the team, but on the days of the match in Sydney, 21–22 February 1867, the scores are blank. He'd disappeared.

'All is well for a couple of days and then things went decidedly pear-shaped,' Josie says.

Charles Lawrence had known Tom Wills from a cricket tour of Ireland a decade earlier and stepped up.

'Charles Lawrence saw the team and he thought they were athletic but he said they needed a bit of coaching,' he says.

He was meticulous in the technique of the game. Under Lawrence's coaching, the Aboriginal team continued to tour by horse and cart around Sydney and New South Wales playing cricket games to raise enough money to get them back home to Victoria's Western District. Charles had promised to help them get home to their families.

But the season had taken its toll. On return at least two of the men died of pneumonia. Another man had died en route.

Still, the dream of a tour to England was very much in everyone's minds. Several new financiers signed on and contracted Charles Lawrence to captain and coach the team. He travelled to Lake Wallace in Edenhope and trained the players for two months before selecting a team.

By late September the men were back on their way to play in Warrnambool, Victoria, the first game on a new tour. This time they were slowly making their way to England.

Rain was persistent in western Victoria, and by all accounts the journey in a large wagon with four horses through the sodden district was eventful. The rain set in early, and they soon became bogged.

The *Warrnambool Examiner* describes another incident when the coachman was ill, so star bowler Yellanach, or Johnny Cuzens, took the reins: 'He drove the horses in full trot up the hill and was thrown off the box onto the hard road, falling with his head on the ground.'

The wheel of the wagon had hit a large stone. Fortunately, he wasn't seriously injured.

It was all completely new and foreign to Charles Lawrence, who got on well with the men, and enjoyed regaling them with stories from his Bible.

'During the trip, Mr Lawrence not having been used to bush travelling was unable to get much sleep, though the blacks made him excellent wigwams and had the fire kept up to his toes,' the newspaper reported. 'The weather was bad and it rained nearly the whole distance.

'Mr Lawrence states that he enjoyed the trip very much, the blacks having been engaged in kangaroo and opossum shooting in the evenings, and occasionally favouring him with a corroboree.'

The newspaper noted, 'They appear like a happy travelling family!'

Even so, Victoria's Aboriginal Protection Board, which had been set up to control the lives of Aboriginal people in that colony, wasn't in favour of the tour. The board's concern was that the men wouldn't be looked after properly, and wouldn't be able to return home.

Despite this, the team wasn't flying too low under the radar. An advertisement in the newspaper on 18 and 19 October 1867 proclaims, 'Lawrence's Aboriginal Cricket Eleven against Eleven of the Corio Cricket Club'.

After the game at Corio in Geelong, Charles Lawrence and team manager William Hayman snuck the men out of Victoria, despite the board's pronouncements. Under the guise of a fishing trip, the team boarded a steamship off Port Phillip Bay and sailed to Wollongong, south of Sydney.

They embarked on another horse-and-cart tour of New South Wales – through Maitland, Singleton, Newcastle, Bathurst and back to Sydney's Albert ground on 4–5 February 1868.

A few days later they caught the wool clipper *Parramatta* and set sail for England. The journey took three months, taking them below South America, across to Africa and up the west coast of Spain and into the port of Plymouth in England.

The Harrow Discovery Centre contains a replica of the boat, and the boomerangs and spears the players put under their bunks for their athletic displays after the games.

In England, the team was well received. It crisscrossed the country, playing 47 games in total over four months. They won 14, lost 14 and drew 19 games.

It was a gruelling schedule and several team members suffered illness – two team members, Balarrimin Nyarringin (Sundown) and Dyalaty Murrimin (Jim Crow), had to return to Australia early, while Brapirr (Bripumyarrimin), known as King Cole, died of tuberculosis and pneumonia in June and was buried in London.

Ngurrinmin (Unaarrimin), or Johnny Mullagh, was the undisputed star of the show. He played 45 games and bowled 1877 overs. He took 245 wickets and made 1698 runs, an average of 24 an innings. His top score was 94. He wasn't paid anything, but received prizes and gifts along with way.

Almost a year to the day after they had sailed for London, they arrived back in Sydney. They were greeted with changing laws. Victoria's 1869 Aboriginal Protection Act ordered that all Indigenous people were to be kept on government reserves or missions.

Ngurrinmin (Unaarrimin/Johnny Mullagh) and bowler Yellanach (Johnny Cuzens) continued to play cricket, including at the MCG.

Ngurrinmin (Unaarrimin/Johnny Mullagh) died at Pine Hill Station in August 1891. At his funeral, mourners placed his bat, and a set of stumps tied in Harrow's cricket club colours, on his coffin. Yangendyinanyuk, or Dick-a-Dick, returned to his home near Mount Elgin station.

It wasn't until many, many years after their deaths that the team's achievements were formally recognised.

One hundred and fifty years on, the photo of the men ahead of their match at the Melbourne Cricket Ground still fills their families with pride.

'I'm aware of the cultural responsibilities which come with that,' Ashley Couzens says. 'For me, as a direct male descendant, I carry our name and continue to honour them, with respect to all our family members and other descendants. Whether it be through work, dance, song, arts, sport or leadership, we have a responsibility to continue this [legacy] and teach our young ones, not just once a year when there is focus on our story, but continuously. This is part of our culture that forever evolves in modern-day Australia.'

Charles Lawrence's great-great-grandson has tried to spread the word ever since he started putting the pieces of the story together all those years ago.

'The story was hard to get out and there was no interest. I found it very difficult to get any interest from anybody,' he says.

In recent times this has changed. Dick-a-Dick's great-great-grandson Richard Kennedy welcomes the fact the team is gaining wider recognition.

'I'm probably disappointed it wasn't done earlier,' he said. 'I think it's great they are being recognised. I hope there's a lot more publicity. It was a special, special event, really.'

Fittingly, a major tour of a men and women's Aboriginal XI squad visited the United Kingdom in 2018 to commemorate the 1868 team, which had toured 150 years earlier. A park was named in honour of King Cole. And the Aboriginal flag was flown at a number of grounds as the teams played. Each player on tour represented one of the original members of the team party, and wore their names emblazoned on their jerseys.

7

Robe

Location: 335 km south of Adelaide, on the Limestone Coast of SA.

Population: 1090

Aired: The Robe episode was filmed to coincide with the start of the 2017 rock lobster fishing season, and the official Blessing of the Fleet in September. It first aired on New Year's Day 2018.

THIS IS A STORY about Robe, a picturesque seaside town in South Australia. But it begins 35 years ago, some 45 minutes to the south-east of here, inland, in the farming community of Furner.

Jacqui Bateman was just a teenager when tornadoes of fire rained down over the farming hamlet during Ash Wednesday, 16 February 1983.

It was late summer and scorching hot. Several years of drought had turned the land into a tinderbox. Fierce winds fanned huge flames. One photo taken from the air captured a tower of fire raging hundreds of metres high.

By the afternoon 14 people were dead, 96 homes were destroyed, hundreds of farms razed and the community was in tatters. Their land was blackened, and the future felt bleak. Some people had lost everything. Their cattle. Their homes. Their partners.

'That was the first time that I'd actually seen a community come together,' Jacqui recalls. 'It was this absolute tragedy, and I remember Furner Sports Club set up a big telecommunications tower. All the electricity and telephones were all wiped out. They set up this big hub and it was amazing. It was the central operation out there. A lot of things focused around that area. Just people helping other people. You see the best and worst of humanity after something like that.'

The thing that's stuck with Jacqui, though, was the action of a group of farmers from Tasmania. They were strangers but had been moved by the plight of the community. On hearing of the stock losses, they banded together and donated a few head of cattle each – and then shipped them to the tired and destroyed farmers of Furner to help them to restock their herds.

'The locals were absolutely incredulous,' Jacqui says. 'Of course, farmers don't say much, do they? But they were all talking about it. God, how's that?

'It was that people could look ahead and rather than give money, give a tangible show of support. It was just that sentiment. To give them something, it meant more, I think. For someone to go to the trouble of actually organising to ship some cattle over.'

Jacqui was only 19 and had been with her boyfriend, Richard, for two years. His family's farm was burned out in the fires and the gift of the cattle was unquantifiable.

It left a lasting impression. Jacqui's still with Richard, 35 years after that fateful day. But she also still carries with her an innate awareness of what a simple act of generosity can do in a time of need.

It was probably there, all these years later, in the deep recesses of her mind, when she felt a pang of something close to helplessness on hearing about suicides in the military. Jacqui hadn't really had any involvement in the military – other than a fascination for guns and building forts and reading adventure magazines as a young girl.

'I was always going to join the police force or the army, but I never did,' she says. 'I've always had this admiration, I guess, for what they do.'

At 17, Jacqui had her heart set on joining the South Australian mounted police. Until she found out she was too young to join. Bored with school in Millicent, she took a year off to get a job, determined to join South Australia's finest the following year.

'It's all I talked about,' she said. 'I knew what I wanted to do. Year 12 wasn't going to have any effect on me. I had 12 months to fill in so I was going to earn some money and at the end of that 12 months I'm out of here.'

But then she met Richard. He was a farmer, with family connections to Furner. She wasn't going anywhere. They've been together ever since.

It was 2014 when Jacqui first recalls being alerted to some of the difficulties faced by our soldiers returning from service. She attended a fundraiser in Canberra and listened to a veteran speak about his struggle to fit back into everyday life. The figures are stark. About 80 returned veterans die by suicide each year in Australia.

It was around Anzac Day, and talkback radio was full of hollow rants about the need to do something. Jacqui felt powerless. It struck a chord, galvanising her to act.

'I thought, it's easy to put your hand into your pocket and pull out $50 and give it to them and feel good and not know where it goes, but I thought, as an individual, how do you actually help someone?' she says. 'I thought, what have I possibly got that I could offer? And I thought, well, I've got a beach house in Robe. If I got in touch with someone and offered that four times a year, that's four people, or four families, that I could help.'

So she hit the phone and also sent emails to a veterans' charity. And waited. And waited some more.

'I thought, I've got this great idea, and they'll get back to me and say it's a great idea,' she says. 'But I never heard back from them.'

It was still on her mind a few months later when a chance meeting provided a breakthrough. She'd been watching her son compete at an athletics event. Near the finish line, a man was standing surrounded by hay bales, herding kids through a mini obstacle course. She spotted a banner for the very veterans' charity she'd been trying to contact.

'I thought, right! And I bowled on up,' she recalls, laughing.

That man was Justin Brown, a returned veteran from conflicts 15 years earlier in Namibia and Cambodia.

'I had a look over and there was a fairly intense look on her face,' he remembers of the encounter. 'I thought, someone wants to have a chat to me.

'She looked at me and she said, I've tried contacting [the charity] and they haven't got back to me,' Justin says. 'And I said to be honest, that's not unheard of. But let's have a chat. I said here's my card and come see me.

'She's a very purposeful kind of person, as you can tell. When she gets something in her focus, that's it. She sticks to it until it's a done thing.'

They got together and chatted. And plotted. And planned. Jacqui and Richard's beach house in Robe provided a much-needed escape from the farm in the blistering summer months, or whenever they needed to get away.

Jacqui thought it could also provide a place of sanctuary to soldiers when it wasn't being used. Jacqui and Justin came up with a program they later called Robe to Recovery, which offers veterans a chance to take a short break in the town, hosted by the community.

Robe knows how to look after visitors. During summer the population swells by tenfold – from 1000 to easily 10,000, as holiday-makers swarm into town and fill the plethora of hotels, caravan parks, restaurants and hideaway beaches.

Tourism is the lifeblood of the place in summer. And in September, it's all about southern rock lobster as Robe's fleet of fishermen set out for their season.

The ocean is beautiful, and bountiful. The distinctive red and white obelisk watches over the waves that splash and crash through eroded rock openings.

About a dozen veterans have been assisted through the Robe to Recovery program since it started inviting people to stay in the off-season, when the town is quiet and the holiday homes empty. Local restaurants and businesses donate vouchers for food or activities, and each provide a little personalised note, thanking the veteran for their service. Some locals might invite the veterans for a game of golf. Or a spot of fishing.

'I was overwhelmed by it,' says Leith Bache, one of the first veterans to visit the town under the program. 'You do feel a sense of pride, obviously, and knowing that people actually recognise it ... just to hear those nice messages thanking you, it makes you feel good.'

Leith had been going through a pretty dark patch when the Robe community stepped in. Years as a combat engineer in the Australian army – serving in Malaysia, East Timor, Papua New Guinea and Afghanistan – had finally taken its toll on his body, and he was medically discharged with a back and neck injury in 2012. The decision sent his world into a spin.

'Initially it was all a bit chaotic, just solely because when you're in [the army], you do feel a bit of a family unit, and once you're out, you're out,' he says.

Having joined the army straight from school, Leith found himself having to start again, with a wife and young son in tow.

'It was a pretty dark time in my life – after doing [some] studies, I spent a good year of solely looking for employment and getting nowhere. I was applying for probably ten or 15 jobs a day and not even getting feedback at all, whatsoever, so I was really struggling with confidence, self-esteem, motivation. Obviously we were struggling financially at the same time, so it was pretty tense at home for that period.'

And then out of the blue, the family received an invitation to spend a few days on the South Australian coast, at Robe. It changed everything.

'We know this is going to help someone who really needs a break,' Jacqui says.

She describes it as the community collectively giving each veteran 'a big hug'.

Justin adds, 'It's amazing what that hug can do for some of the toughest people in the country.'

Many military people feel a bit abandoned when they leave the military, Justin says. Often they don't want to go.

'There's no fanfare,' he explains. 'There's no real formal exit for them. And those who have been medically discharged are often leaving against their will. They don't want to go and they feel a bit abandoned. They lose that sense of purpose. Their sense of self-worth.

'They often feel that what they've done didn't really mean anything and no one knows they were there or what they were doing. Whereas when they come down here, just a simple card or a gift or a letter that says thank you for what you have done for us – that just goes a long way. It's a really simple gesture but it means a hell of a lot.'

Many other veterans' programs focus on more structured psychiatric support, but Robe to Recovery is very different.

'I think this is a unique program. I don't think it's been done anywhere,' Justin says. 'I think the program that Jacqui conceptualised was really about more of the heart; was more about connecting with the human aspect of it. And from that comes better results than clinical support. Because it's genuine. It hasn't come out of a book. It's come directly from the people who have donated their goods and services.

'The community has basically opened its arms to say welcome and thank you for what you have done. Rather than a psychologist saying, how do you feel about that? Let's go back to the thing that might have been the trigger for your PTSD. Whereas the community here are not sitting there interrogating. We accept you are struggling because of your service. But what can we do to help you out?'

Veterans' organisations estimate one in ten Australian Defence Force personnel suffer physical or psychological injuries from active service.

For Leith and his family, the trip to Robe was a reinvigorating experience. They've returned for a second break since then, and Leith has found employment.

'It gave us a chance to sort of freshen up a bit,' he said. 'Obviously, at the end of the day we had to go back to the reality of what our life was, but it just gave us that period where we could pretend we weren't in that position and we just got to come here. It's a temporary relief, that's what it is, but sometimes that's all you sort of need.'

Since the *Back Roads* program aired an episode on the Robe to Recovery program in 2018, Jacqui and Justin have been inundated with offers of support and messages from veterans and their families asking how they can visit.

'We are still feeling our way a bit, but we've got some big ideas,' Jacqui says.

Five other towns have come on board to offer their own veterans' getaways – Mittagong in New South Wales; Cobden, Phillip Island and the Mornington Peninsula in Victoria; and Moonta Bay on South Australia's Yorke Peninsula.

They've created a template of their Robe to Recovery program so other towns can copy it.

'It's still a work in progress,' Jacqui says.

Justin says Jacqui's passion is the reason the program has evolved and grown the way it has.

'I've been nothing but happy to support it right from the very outset because I know that while the benefit it provides is difficult to measure, you can see it, and you can hear it,' he says. 'You can see the change in people after they come down. Seeing them 12 months later and seeing the improvement that it's made to them is really quite remarkable. And while it's only a small part of the jigsaw puzzle, I think it's really, really important and really effective.

'And the more programs like this that we can create around the country, it just dovetails nicely into all the other support services that are being provided – the professional medical services, the advocacy and social welfare that's available in other organisations. But this is just as special. It's really just that community support and recognition piece that is missing.'

Jacqui is thrilled that other towns are coming on board. But she's still focused. And resolute.

'Who would have thought it would have grown to this?' she says. 'I'm beside myself with how it's grown. I always thought I'd love to make this national, but how do you do it? There's all this untold support for our defence forces. It's just simmering away there, but people don't know how to help.

'As an individual it's hard to have an impact, but collectively as a community it's so powerful. You can do so much.'

8
Mundulla

Location: 283 km south-east of Adelaide, South Australia.

Population: 436

Aired: The episode on Mundulla was the first episode in the second series of *Back Roads*. It aired in November 2016.

SUNLIGHT IS STREAMING THROUGH the windows. It's going to be a hot day; sweltering. It already is.

Beads of sweat are forming on Vida Maney's forehead. It's furrowed in concentration as she furiously rolls clumps of sultana-speckled dough into plump, even balls. She's doing it all with one hand. Tearing and kneading. Rolling. Repeating. Her left hand, injured at birth, is supporting her against the wooden bench.

'If you'll excuse me, I'll keep working because the pressure's on,' she apologises. 'I've got a lot of entries to get in.'

Vida has a direct, matter-of-fact manner. It's no surprise to learn she was a school teacher many years ago. Vida is quite forthright. Always. But her energy is infectious and vibrant, and her stamina unshakable.

'My mother didn't like us to sit around reading as we'd like to,' Vida explains. 'I probably would have liked to take advantage of my disability, but there was no way she would allow that. If I said, "I can't do that", she'd say, "try harder", and that was her attitude pretty well to life in general, I think – try harder.'

It's a mantra that has clearly seeped into Vida's subconscious, judging from the output of her remarkable life thus far. And it goes some way towards explaining her current predicament.

It's 2016 and *Back Roads* is visiting Vida as she prepares for the annual Mundulla Show, in just a couple of days' time. The show is in its one-hundred-and-sixth year and Vida has been an enthusiastic show entrant for more than half that time.

But this year she's set the bar so high there's not a second to lose. She's determined to prepare 81 individual entries for the show – one for each year she's been alive – across the categories of cut flowers, pot plants, ginger beer, preserves and yeast cookery.

Her fingers move at lightning speed as she breaks off another piece of dough with her right hand and rolls it around and a round, folding it onto itself, poking in an errant sultana, and transforming it into a show-worthy yeast bun. All within a few seconds. It's then added to the baking tray with the others.

She's wearing round, clear-rimmed glasses, and a collared aqua T-shirt, with barely a puff of flour on it.

'I'm noted for my yeast buns but don't always win,' Vida remarks. 'There could be somebody else knock me off but I always enter and have a go. Sometimes they are better than others. We yeast cooks always say these are not as good as the last batch I made. But we always live in hope.'

She fetches a large glass jar from the fridge behind her and sets it on the bench. It contains a thick white sludge, coagulated around the rim. 'I use old-fashioned potato water yeast,' she explains. 'I've had a batch on the go for a long time.'

Fifty years, in fact.

'I've probably changed the bottle a few times – it gets a bit grotty, as you can see. It all sticks to the side.'

Vida explains that her problems with the left side of her body stem from a brain injury she received from the use of forceps at her birth.

'I'm very much a one-handed person,' she says. 'My left hand and my left leg are not much good to me. It's a very minor disability but it's probably getting a bit worse as I get older, as a lot of things do. It's as if I had a stroke when I was born. And I'm very lucky it's as minor as it is, and more than lucky that I had very sensible parents.

'I was born in 1935 – times were pretty tough at that time. My dad was a farm manager and not a farm owner at that stage. But I had treatment from the time I was two, so I was very fortunate.'

Vida grew up in South Australia's south-east, the youngest of six children. When she was eight she lived in a children's home for 20 months as she underwent treatment to improve the use of her arm and leg. The treatment involved wearing a short iron cast on her leg – but it didn't hurt, she says.

She moved to the Mundulla farming district two weeks before her 18th birthday, as a new teacher at a one-teacher school called Cannawigra. It was 1953. Soon after, she met her husband, John, who right now is sitting quietly, keeping well out of the fray and sporadically dozing on the lounge next to their daughter's brown terrier, Molly.

They've lived on their property, Panaroo (meaning 'little place'), for 12 years, having lived beside their drapery shop in Mundulla for 45 years. John later confides that Vida wanted to change the name for many years, because of the potential for confusion with a town to the north, Pinnaroo.

'One of the few wins I've ever had,' he grins.

Vida and John will celebrate their sixtieth wedding anniversary in 2018.

Mundulla is a hamlet surrounded by rich agricultural country away from the main highways, in South Australia, close to the Victorian border. The road into town is lined with majestic gum trees which form a canopy overhead. Mundulla's three main businesses – a historic pub, general store and gift shop – sit at a T-junction in the heart of the community. There are no traffic lights. Or roundabouts.

'We haven't changed a great deal in the 140-odd years since we were first proclaimed a town in 1873,' Vida says.

Naturally, Vida, and John, were on the town centenary committee when that milestone was achieved. The couple have always been stalwarts of the community. They still are. Between them they've racked up decades and decades of service. At the local hall, the football club, the progress association, the schools, compiling the community newsletter, and the Mundulla Show.

It's a place that values tradition. The local debutante ball has been running for more than 50 years. The show has been running for more than a hundred.

'We mightn't have big industries but we've got almost everything we need,' Vida says. 'We're a community that works together to support each other. We've got a strong sense of community and strong values of community. Everybody helps everybody else.'

Vida's received an Order of Australia for her service to the visually impaired and the community. She's long been a writer and local historian. Perhaps influenced by her early start as a school teacher, she's been writing children's books for decades.

'I'm a one-fingered typist and I'm a self-taught anything to do with computer skills,' Vida says.

Even so, she's created thousands of tactile books for visually impaired children around Australia over the past four decades. 'It's the most rewarding thing I've ever done in all my life,' she says.

It was around 1980 when Vida read about women making similar books. She was spurred into action.

'I couldn't put it out of my mind because they asked the question, have you ever thought that a blind child can't enjoy a picture book?' she says. 'They can have stories read to them, through the wonders of braille they can learn to read, but they can't have a picture book. And little kids love picture books. So that really stuck in my mind.'

Vida was president of the Uniting Church ladies group at the time. 'I thought we've had travel talks and we've had cake decorating. We've had flower arranging. I'll knock their socks off: we'll have something totally different.'

No other groups in South Australia were making tactile books at the time, but Vida was encouraged to give it a go.

'I was sure we'd get six books done. I mean, I had no idea. I'd done almost no preparation. And one of them was very simple; we called it *Bacon for Breakfast*. Tom didn't want to get up because he knew if he got up he'd have to take off his pyjamas and fold them. He'd have to put on his jeans. He'd have to put on his shirt and button it up. He'd have to do his hair with the brush and comb. He'd have to clean his teeth with the toothbrush. So we just had pyjamas and toothbrush and things like that as their illustration. But Mum called out, "Bacon for breakfast!" so Tom quickly put on all his clothes, dashed into the kitchen and sat down for breakfast. We got a lot of feedback from the school for the visually-impaired – the kids really enjoyed that one.'

The process was much more complicated than even Vida had anticipated. The books needed special paper. And a braille typist.

Over the years Vida has co-opted different community groups into helping her, illustrating each page of the stories with fabric or felt sewn into different animal shapes or objects. She's written hundreds of different simple stories, producing about 3000 books in total.

'At one stage, we were doing 15 copies of every book,' Vida says. 'They went to schools for the blind all over Australia.'

It's slowed down considerably now, as there is less need, thanks to new technology, she says.

'A couple of years ago I thought, no, I'm finished. I'm not going to do any more. And then I went out to the shed and I came across a box with lots of camels and a dozen kangaroos and a hundred ducks and thought, I'll do the books until I finish them up. And I like doing teddy bears, and I've always got a bag of something by my chair, although through the summer I haven't done much because my hands are too sticky and sweaty.'

It's always been hot in summer in Mundulla, since she first moved to the district six decades ago.

Vida met John soon after she arrived. He was the brother of one of her teammates on the local women's hockey team, and he drove them to take part in an interleague match. As they took to the field, he agreed to look after Vida's wristwatch.

'The kids say to me, Mum, you were out to hook him and what's what – the day I met John was the day he held my watch. So romantic,' she laughs.

They got married a few years later – in 1958 – and moved into the drapery store Maneys of Mundulla, which John at that time owned with his brother. It was much more than a drapery store, though, Vida says. It had everything. From books to toys, haberdashery, stationery and clothing.

'I'm a very untidy person and, really, it's difficult to run a shop and keep it tidy,' she says. 'Our kids always said as they were growing they were always dressed in shelf-warmers – the things that wouldn't sell.'

The couple owned the store for 45 years before selling it. Vida ran it for much of that time. John was a painter and decorator.

Today, the vintage shopfront is captured in a large embroidery wall hanging in Vida's kitchen. 'Maneys of Mundulla' is framed by rows of buttons sewn into a patchwork design. Above it hangs a colourful artwork displaying six child handprints of various sizes – in white, grey, black, yellow, red and blue paint. They belong to the couple's six grandchildren.

Three of Vida and John's four children still live in Mundulla. It's one of the noticeable traits about Mundulla. It's a small place. But when people leave, they usually return.

'I think a lot of people leave Mundulla but their heart stays here and they come back again,' Vida says. 'It's happened in lots of families.'

She puts it down to the strength of the community, bound together by a solid football club, enduring show society and intergenerational friendships.

'I like the fact that I can go down the street and lots of mums and dads will say, hello Mrs Maney, and the kids will say, hello Vida, because they've met me when I've gone to talk with them at school about something or other. I think that's lovely. To think they think of me as a friend.'

This year, at the 2016 Mundulla Show, Vida's been encouraging 15-year-old student Amy Steer to try and seize her crown for 'most show entries'. Vida's won it at least 15 times. Amy's submitted hundreds of entries – in cooking, photography and metalwork, plus a quilt she made with her grandmother.

'I just enjoy putting in entries in the show, just to have something to do for the show,' Amy says.

It's all part of Vida's cunning plan to ensure the Mundulla Show's longevity well into the future.

'She's got years of showing ahead of her,' Vida says. 'Oh yes, I'm ready to hand over to somebody else.'

Participation in the Mundulla Show is generational for the Maney family. Vida's daughter Liz Goossens delivers basket upon basket of her mother's entries on show day.

'All the family's involved – nieces, nephews, and everybody has a job on the day,' Liz says. 'And we love the excitement really. She keeps promising it's going to be the last year but each time it comes around we are doing it again.'

Vida's granddaughter McKeeley Maney has been volunteering since she was ten years old. She's in charge of the cookery section.

'Why do I want a job? Hmm, you could say that I'm a Maney and you have to have a job on show day,' she laughs. 'I just love it. Hearing the judge's comments every year are just so interesting. I'm finding out about how each and every cake is cooked and what makes a champion cake.

'There's a lot of fear that shows will die out and so you've got people like us who are really passionate about seeing that they will keep going and will stay strong in our communities.'

Country shows are the lifeblood of rural towns like Mundulla.

'It puts the district on show but it really is about the community working together,' Vida says. 'We get involved because we are proud of the community, but also because over the years the show has had wonderful support and we don't want to see it fade away. It's been an integral part of our family's life but also an integral part of the community, with many people working to make it a success.'

Vida handed over the crown for most show entries to Amy Steer, but by 2018, at 83, she is still putting up a good fight.

Amy Steer won the most entries again last year in 2017, Vida confides with a smile. Her younger sister was runner-up.

It's a couple of weeks from 2018's show day, and two years since the *Back Roads* episode on Mundulla was first broadcast.

Vida says most of the town watched the episode together at a local sports club.

'I was absolutely horrified because I had no idea there was going to be so much of that crippled-up, bent-over old woman,' she says. 'And the fact is it wasn't me at all: it was my mother. And I couldn't get over that, how much like my mum I've become.'

She's busy preparing her show entries again, and is planning on making her ginger beer later today.

'But I'm not too sure whether I'll have buns or not because my oven is out of action and we've got a new stove sitting out there, waiting to be installed,' Vida says. 'I will have entries but they are all saying to me, not as many, Mum, you know you're much slower.

'I just turned 83. I reckon I might only have about 70 entries this year.'

9

Marree

Location: 674 km north of Adelaide, South Australia.

Population: 101

Aired: The episode on the Oodnadatta Track, encompassing the towns of Marree, Oodnadatta and William Creek, was the first in the series to air in two parts, as the third and fourth episodes of *Back Roads* Series Three. They aired on 11 and 18 December 2017.

A CROWD IS STANDING in front of two large steel structures, and lined along a low cyclone fence. There's a hushed murmur of anticipation. Cans of beer, and mobile phones, are at the ready. Not that you'd get a signal out here. It's hundreds of kilometres from anywhere. In the middle of Australia's big, dusty heart.

Back Roads has travelled to Marree, a tiny town in South Australia's far north, for the 2017 Camel Cup races. A row of camels, adorned with saddles in a patchwork of bright colours, stand together in a pen.

Those spectators who aren't waiting for a race are lined up at a window, literally a hole in the wall. 'BEER TICKETS', says the sign. One man has two small dogs by his side. Bookmakers are taking odds on camels with names like Hay Bale, Hussy's Glow and Breaker of Chains. Money changes hands at a quick pace: 'Five each way on number one, thanks.'

'He's a bit skittish, this one,' a handler nods as he leads a camel down the track. 'He only stopped bucking in the last two races.'

Four camels are led in a circle, one by one, for the crowd, which whoops in appreciation.

'Here we go, we are turning around. The 2017 Marree Camel Cup. Look for the puff of dust,' the MC announces from a box up high. 'Wouldn't it be wonderful if we had mobile coverage in Marree – you could ring all your mates and tell them where we are.'

A loud starter gun jolts the participants into action. With a cloud of red dust, four camels begin awkwardly lumbering down the Marree Racecourse. One at the back is going the wrong way.

'Here we go … They're having a proper go, anyway … She's going to be close.'

The jockeys sit so far down the back of the camels, they look as if they're about to slip off. They're in silk shirts. Green numbers are also spray-painted on the camels' long necks.

'Hook 'em up, here he is. Old hook 'em up!'

The crowd whoops. Wheeyhey.

The Camel Cup's been a popular event for decades. It started 25 years ago in recognition of the town's unique heritage, a celebration of all things camel in honour of the scores of camel drivers who travelled to this remote part of the world 150 years ago and made it their home.

Largely forgotten now, they forged new paths, trekking thousands of kilometres with chains of camels, some 70 beasts long, carrying goods weighing several hundred kilograms. They helped build Australia's earliest infrastructure – the Overland Telegraph, a railway to Alice Springs and more. And they supplied goods to pastoral stations in harsh, remote country, returning with bales of wool for sale. They helped drive the earliest expeditions through the outback, on treacherous journeys of scientific and geographic discovery. In all there were at least 2000 camel drivers across Australia from the 1860s, and around 20,000 camels.

'A lot of people in the world don't know about the traditions, about the bush and what they've done,' says Camel Cup organiser Robert Khan. 'They opened most of this country up because the horses couldn't do it, you know, in the heat. So they came out and did it all with camels. They carted railway lines, wool and the Overland Telegraph for the country. I think without them we would have been in a bad way.'

Robert's father was a cameleer. Mormin Khan left school when he was eight and walked with a string of 70 camels to Birdsville. It was 1915.

'Most of his brothers, they worked from daylight till dark.' He never thought of following in his father's footsteps, though? 'No, no. It seemed too hard for me.'

Marie Williams is also at the Camel Cup. She's trackside, handing out ribbons, and hugs, to winners of the Afghan Memorial Cup.

'Who came second?' she asks, before putting a red ribbon around a boy with a black cap.

Marie's also a descendant of the cameleers. Of perhaps the most famous of them: a man named BJ the Faithful, Bejah Dervish.

'I feel very proud of my heritage. When we were kids we didn't realise how important things were, but as we've become older we've just learned to appreciate it a lot more,' she says. 'He was an amazing man. He stood tall and he had a silk turban and used to wear what we used to call bloomers like trousers.'

She no longer lives in Marree, but still owns the 125-year-old house her grandfather built.

'I didn't want to lose that connection. When I retired I put a new little house in front of it so I go up there quite regularly. There's still several of the main people who lived in Marree; their houses are still standing there. I just love the peace.'

It's where Marie grew up with her four siblings, and three pet camels. Marie named hers Orange 'because she had a nice colour'.

'When the old Afghan cameleers came here, they built mud houses,' she says. 'And then gradually built iron houses, corrugated iron houses. We've added to it over the years. We had lots of happy memories of this place, and that's why we keep coming back.'

It's wide, open country, surrounded by distant red-brown hills. The skies are big. An occasional tree provides shade from the unforgiving sun.

Long before the cameleers came, for thousands of years the traditional custodians, the Arabana people, traded with neighbouring communities along the Oodnadatta Track.

Despite being called 'Afghan' cameleers, the camel drivers came from different parts of the Asian subcontinent. Many cameleers left after completing two- or three-year contracts. Their families were back home and they weren't allowed to bring them to Australia. But others stayed and had families here.

Marie's grandfather Bejah Dervish was born in 1862 in Baluchistan, in what is now Pakistan. She says he spoke Arabic, and learned English when he arrived in Australia, around 1890. He settled in Marree, buying three pieces of land. In 1909 Bejah Dervish married a widow with eight children, Amelia Shaw. They had a son together, Marie's father, Abdul Jubbar (Jack).

The cameleers worked very hard, and could be away on remote expeditions for months at a time.

'I've seen a photo of a camel taking a piano to a station,' Marie says. 'The Afghans looked after their camels like pets. They were all named and they knew every camel – it wasn't like they used them and just discarded them.'

The idea of using camels to transport goods was first raised in the 1830s. Australia's vast inland desert was deemed too harsh for horses or bullock transportation. It wasn't until 1860, though, that the first cameleers arrived, along with 24 camels, for the ill-fated Burke and Wills expedition.

After that, the cameleers and camels arrived in small numbers. They were brought in initially on contracts to transport wool and other goods for South Australia's pastoralists. Within a few years the cameleers had started their own businesses importing camels and moving goods. Some became hawkers. They helped build the famous railway that ran from Port Augusta, through Marree, to Alice Springs. When it opened in 1929 it was named the Ghan in their honour.

'Most people who'd worked in the camel industry, and their sons, they all had a job in the railways back then,' Marie says.

The track was diverted in 1980, and today the modern railway bypasses the town. It changed the town.

'Everybody had to shift. Most people went to Port Augusta, but, you know, it makes me wonder sometimes if the railway line did still run through here what Marree would look like, because it was a big town then. But of course, there isn't much here any more.'

The cameleers played a significant role in exploring Australia's vast regions. In 1896 Marie's grandfather Bejah Dervish led 20 camels on an expedition through the Great Sandy Desert for South Australian explorer Lawrence Wells. It was named the Calvert Expedition, after the mining magnate who had commissioned it.

'He became known as BJ the Faithful because he went back. A man had been lost and he wouldn't leave until they found him,' Marie says.

It was an incredible journey. Dervish displayed great devotion to the camels under his care. He refused to eat if his camels had no feed. Two men died on the journey, and the expedition leader, Lawrence Wells, presenting Dervish with a compass in recognition of his service, said, 'We would never have got through alive without him'.

There were a number of expeditions. BJ Dervish was again approached more than 40 years later. He sent his son Jack (Abdul), Marie's father, instead. In 1939 Jack led 19 camels on a scientific expedition by geologist Cecil Madigan to investigate the flora and fauna of the Simpson Desert.

It was around that time that Jack met his future wife. Bebe Norah Fazulla used to write letters for the Afghan cameleers in Broken Hill.

'She was educated, whereas a lot of the old Afghans weren't, so she would write their business letters for them,' Marie says. 'If someone was selling a camel to somebody, or saddles. That type of thing.'

One of her clients decided to set her up with Jack. They wrote letters to each other for years, and married in 1942.

When Marie was small, Marree was a bustling railway town. It's where a lot of the second generation of camel drivers worked after the industry was replaced by motorised transport from the late 1920s.

'Growing up as a child in Marree was tops,' she recounts to *Back Roads* host Heather Ewart, seated on a bench made from an old railway sleeper outside the old family home. 'We all went to school together, whether we were Afghans, white kids, Aboriginal kids. We were all good friends and we still are.'

The house appears to be made of tin, and the dusty backyard opens out onto a flat, dry expanse that stretches all the way to the horizon.

'This used to be a house where everybody came. All the old Afghans would gather at the house and they'd sit outside with a fire bucket, and sit around smoking. We had a date plantation down there. I remember my grandfather would never let us go near his date palms. If the kids came, he'd chase them away until they were ripe enough.

'We all lived here in what they called Ghan Town.'

Marree was divided in half by the railway track. The white people – the police officer, postman and shopkeeper – lived on the south side. The Afghans were on the north side, alongside the Aboriginals, in Ghan Town.

Marie says the geographical divisions have disappeared. 'Everybody's all in one now, regardless of who you are.'

It was a different story when Marie's parents were younger and camel driving was being phased out. The Afghans were disliked, she says: 'The wider population didn't really like the Afghans because they were making lots of money. When trucks came, they were trying to get rid of them.

'They put a ninepence levy on each camel. Because of the train, and the trucks, there wasn't much use for the camels, so they let them go. That's why there are lots of camels all over Australia now.'

The cameleers adhered to their faith. They built Australia's first mosque in Marree, although there's nothing left of it now. A number are buried in the Muslim section on the local cemetery.

Marie remembers her grandfather was a strict Muslim, but her parents were more flexible. When she was an adult she converted to Catholicism.

'Mum and Dad were very strict with us and brought us up to be good citizens wherever we went,' she recalls. 'We were brought up as Muslims, but my father used to make sure that we went to every church group that came here, so we got a pretty good understanding of most of the religions. Mum and Dad sent us to the whole lot because they wanted us to be like the other kids, I guess.'

One of the main Afghan traditions that remains strong in Marree is the curries.

'Everybody loves curries and the chapattis,' Marree says. 'We all make different kinds, but we all love curries.'

It's the day after the Camel Cup. Many of the descendants of the early cameleers have returned for the races. But it's just the prelude to the main event: a huge curry night.

It's held up the road from Marie's house, at the home of a childhood friend. Another of Afghan descent. In a house once known as 'Deano's Casino'.

'Everybody makes curries and chapattis and everybody's welcome to go there,' Marie says. 'It's a really big thing for everybody to meet, and greet, and eat curry. It starts about lunchtime and goes all night.'

An old Afghan song is being played on a piano accordion. People are watching from long bench seats surrounding a campfire in the backyard.

'Come on, you blokes down the back, come up and have a feed.'

There's nine large silver saucepans with lids on a table nearby. Each is filled with a different curry, in an array of colours. The old friends sit around the fire and share stories and a laugh. Just like their pioneering ancestors used to.

10

Ceduna

Location: 773 km north-west of Adelaide, on the west coast of the Eyre Peninsula.

Population: 2157

Aired: The *Back Roads* episode on Ceduna was the first to air in the series. It premiered on Monday 29 November 2015.

CRAIG STINEAR IS BENDING down, marking short lines with a can of white spray paint. Every few minutes he straightens up, raises his brown Akubra in the air and grins as a hefty road train thunders past, blaring its horn in greeting. Craig – or Oolie to his mates – knows most of the old-time truck drivers who pass him out here on Highway One.

It's 2015 and *Back Roads* is visiting Oolie in his 'office' – a 620-kilometre stretch of bitumen that runs the length of South Australia's Great Australian Bight.

The reddish-brown highway stretches like a wave over the landscape, far into the distance. It's bordered by occasional clumps of bushes and a stream of powerlines. Stubby white poles with reflectors stand patiently at intervals. Highway One traverses the Nullarbor Plain, all the way to the Western Australian border.

'I'm just mucking around out here,' Oolie says, his spray can in hand.

He's standing on the side of a stretch of highway about 20 kilometres west of Ceduna.

'They've got a big hopscotch competition in Adelaide later on in the year and I've got to draw a practice course out here for the hopscotch,' he says. 'All these international people are coming from around the world and they want to practise somewhere, so we thought this patch of road would be a good spot to practise on.'

Oolie's expression is deadpan and his sense of humour so dry it's difficult to tell if he's joking.

'Dinkum,' he says. Then pauses. 'No, that was a bit of piffle. Scratch that,' he shrugs, slightly embarrassed. 'I'm just finding a bit of work for the men. There's a few defects along the road here, and I'm just marking them out and they will come along later and patch them up.'

Oolie is a man of few words. But then they come, they are often surprising and waggish. It's impossible to know if Oolie's jocularity stems, in part, from his decades working in isolation on the highways. Or from the extraordinary things he's witnessed.

Perhaps his larrikin streak is the reason he's been able to stay in the job, and enjoy it, for so long. Oolie's seen pretty much everything in his 34 years working on the remote highway. He leads a team of workers who maintain it and dispose of the rubbish in the parking bays, and the abundant road kill. He also cleans up after horrific road crashes, as well as maintaining and replacing the signs, and, as we now know, patching up flaws in the road surface.

Oolie clocks up about 70,000 kilometres driving along the road each year. He meets a lot of people along the way. Many are full of questions. But he freely admits with a grin that he might not always have the right answers.

'Is it always this windy? Are the flies always here? Where are the camels?' He lists the regular ones. 'Sometimes they look like they're asking for a little fib or something, so you give them a bit of a twisted view of where they are or where they should be going; add to their confusion.

'Not everyone gets the truth. Some deserve it, some just don't deserve the truth, you know. Never tell them you don't know. All they want is an answer – it doesn't matter what it is. You work out how gullible they are and you give them an answer that fits their personality.'

He's seen all sorts of people, in all manner of situations. A number are clearly unprepared for the outback or their journey through it. Some are ignorant about the risks, and a few are oblivious to the dangers they pose, both to themselves and others, by their actions.

'You know, probably my biggest regret in the job was never carrying a camera from day one,' he says. 'Just to take photos of some of the loads, the oversized stuff and people getting through on monocycles. I've seen people pushing a hospital bed through and riding horses and camels through and whatever, in different stages of being pissed and stoned.

'Only a couple of weeks ago I was up here at Nullarbor in front of the roadhouse and a guy pulled up and he wanted to know which way Melbourne was, and I thought, well, there's only one road here. I just pointed east and said, east is short cut, west is long cut.

'I've met some really great people and I've met some people you probably wouldn't travel too far to ever meet again.'

Oolie is dressed in a blue shirt and pants, and a bright orange vest with yellow stripes. He's full of stories. On every topic.

'I've seen people out there with flat tyres,' he says. 'Out west of Nullarbor one time, a couple of guys in a car, they had a flat tyre and the spare was flat. I pulled up to see if they were all right, and they flattened the tyre east of Broken Hill somewhere – they'd been driving for 1500 kilometres through a lot of towns with a flat tyre. They thought they'd get it repaired when they got to Perth.'

If there's children involved, he'll do whatever he can to help.

'I fixed a car up one day, had to muck around with the points and get it going. It was about 45 degrees and they had a little baby in the car,' he says. 'I just felt sorry for the little kid. I got the car going and I said, it's not running real good but it will get you to Nullarbor Roadhouse, anyway, and there you've got water and aircon; there you can look after a baby.

'Another time I was driving along and there was a car on the side of the road and a little kid standing there. I just went past and I thought, shit, I reckon there's someone laying in the bushes and I went back there and this kid was there and there was this woman lying in the bushes. I said what's going on here, mate? This kid he was probably only 10 or 12 years old and he said mum got out of the car and she fell over.

'I bloody thought, shit, she's had a stroke or a heart attack or something, so I checked her out. She was still breathing but I thought I'd better pick her up and put her in the car, get her out of the bush, anyway. Bloody hell, she just stunk like a brewery carthorse's fart. She was just pissed. Driving across Australia. I felt so sorry for this poor little kid. You've got to be smarter than that. Just bloody unbelievable.

'Over the years you forget. Once I saw a couple of blokes pull up, and I don't know if they were known to each other or what, but they were just having an all-in brawl on the side of the road,' he continues. 'They slid over the edge in prickles and were swinging at each other, and it looked like they were enjoying themselves.'

In the remote outback, the realities of life and death are pronounced.

'I've seen a few cyclists. They get wiped out up there by the road trains and stuff,' he says. 'I've seen them dying out there. I've seen them getting created out there. We pulled in a parking bay there one day, me and another guy. Well, a dad was checking a mum's oil,' he guffaws. We didn't interrupt them. We just changed the rubbish bin and did what we had to do and kept on going.

'The downside is probably the prangs. A lot of fatal prangs. And to sort the mess out. Scrape up the bits and pieces. Up there there's no one else around, we're it. The ambulance will be there. Nowadays they've got SES, but years ago they never had that. They just had the ambulance, the coppers and it was just us. You just done what you did to sort the mess out. Some of that wasn't too good but it was just part of the job.'

The paint can in his hand rattles as he acknowledges another vehicle passing through with a slight wave. 'He's a local sparky from Penong,' Oolie explains.

Oolie has lived in Ceduna his entire life. His nickname comes from a local Aboriginal word that means 'little kid'.

The depot headquarters is on the outskirts of town. It contains a large shed, full of tools and random road signs stacked in a row against the wall. An assortment of signs are hung next to each other: 'P14', 'N12', 'N154'. A yellow circle 'slow' sign is upside down. The air-conditioned demountable office is about 50 metres away, closer to the highway.

For Oolie and his team, one of the biggest frustrations is people stealing road signs as souvenirs. Some people even bring angle grinders to cut them off their posts.

'People collect all our animal signs: camel, kangaroo, wombats,' he says. 'Camel and wombats, they love them. They'll get the sign down one way or another if they really want it.'

When Oolie first started in the early 1980s, after Australia won the America's Cup yacht race, it was the little green and gold highway markers that kept disappearing. Oolie's gang punched 'bullet holes' into them – much to the chagrin of work gangs further down the road.

'They were going off like hot cakes and we used to just poke a hole in them with a centre punch, make it look like a bullet hole or whatever and they'd travel down the road to the next gang's area and steal them from there,' he says.

Oolie says he was born 'across the road' from the depot.

'I haven't gone far,' he laughs. 'I live down the road that way, 300 yards. And for a fair while I lived down the road that way, 300 yards.' He points the other way. 'I'm just a local. I don't know how many generations. Lots. Before my time.'

Oolie describes his hometown of Ceduna as 'the hub of the universe for people that are born and bred here'.

'I can't see myself going anywhere else as long as when I get older I've got enough strength and health to be able to pull a razorfish out of the mud and wind my tinny back on the trailer, and catch a feed of fish. That's all I want,' he muses.

His favourite spot, though, is the Nullarbor.

'I enjoy working up Nullarbor, mainly in autumn when it's nice, calm, balmy days,' he says. 'It's a good climate. It's just peaceful. No one to annoy you. You've got no mobile phone or nothing, or back then you never had, anyway. Yeah, I just love being out in the open. I don't think I want to work anywhere else.

'Out on the plain, it's beautiful. Most people just speed through. I saw wedge-tail eagle chicks last year. They were just alongside the highway. There's a lot of stuff if you keep your eyes open.

'Some days when you're up the Bight, you're having smoko or lunch, you look out and you've got whales swimming past and you think some people probably sit in an office in the city and they don't see this sort of stuff.

'Mind you, there's some days you wouldn't want to be out there too – the wind will blow the milk out of your coffee there on a good day.

'But it's a place to work and someone's got to do it.'

He joined the roads department in 1981, at the age of 22.

'For me it's just a job, you know. I enjoy it – I probably wouldn't have been here so long if I didn't enjoy it,' he says. 'You're out in the bush. I just don't know that I'd like to work in a town or in a shed and go to the same place every day – here you roam around a bit.'

Oolie was working on various farms when a bloke asked him if he wanted to join the roads team. At first, he was reluctant.

'At that stage I didn't because it was raining and it looked all right on the farms and I was having fun and then by September it turned into a bit of a dry year, so I thought, oh well, I might as well have a crack at this job – and I'm still here.

'Years go by; you don't really notice it much, you know. Days roll into weeks and into months, I suppose, and then you get some annual leave, and then you go away and you come back all freshened up and have another crack at it.'

Believe it or not, Oolie loves to go on driving holidays with his family – wife Sai and daughter Emily – when he's not working.

'I can't wait to retire and just drive around Australia at bloody 40 kilometres an hour filling up rubbish bins in parking bays and giving everyone the shits,' he laughs.

'We've just been up the beach for a couple of nights for the weekend with a couple of Ceduna people, we just sat by a fire and had a sheep-tasting ceremony. And a beer-tasting ceremony. Yeah, had some chops and some cans.'

It's now early 2018, and Oolie is sitting in the demountable office at the depot. He has retirement on his mind. But not yet.

'I've got to do another four years, three years, something. It just depends on super,' he says.

His desk is a mess of papers. The department is closing down the gangs and replacing them with private contractors.

'I'm the only survivor,' he says.

'I'm not real sure what my new job is. I've got a couple of good workers here. I am trying to get them sorted, you know. A lot of the men will just swing into the private contract. Once everyone is sorted, I'll worry about my job.'

Once he starts his new role, Oolie will oversee the work on the roads. His patch will expand to two or three thousand kilometres, from the Western Australia border through to Port Augusta and Port Lincoln.

'It's been a good way of life for the best part of 40 years,' he reflects. 'I enjoyed it. I was just hoping I could have seen it out as part of a team. It's the end of an era.'

He's noticed a few changes in the three years since the *Back Roads* episode aired. And a few people have noticed him. The road's busier, for starters.

'There's a lot more grey nomads. People are retired with money now and they are just travelling more,' he says. 'Our parking bays get a bit of a hammering out there because everyone's got shower and toilet in their caravans.

'I pulled up there one day, a couple of ladies had trouble with the rope on a trailer, and I pulled up and tied a load down for them. I was walking across the road and this old duck looks at me and she says, I know you!' Oolie laughs deeply. 'I looked at her and she said, you were on TV. And I said, oh yeah, I suppose.'

Typically, a day on the road involves a lot of road kill – often discovered in the same areas; when unfortunate motorists meet unlucky camels, wombats and kangaroos.

'I saw a truck take out 14 [camels] with one hit once – shortened the life of the truck a bit in a matter of seconds,' Oolie said, hands in pockets. 'Over the years there's been quite a few hit. I think sometimes in the cold weather they [the animals] will go and camp out on the road and sleep there, where it's warm, or they feed along the road in the droughts, where there's a bit of green picking.'

He disposes of the flyblown carcasses by dragging them off to the side of the road, and letting the eagles and dingoes 'clean up'.

The biggest problem at the moment, though, is wombats. Dozens are getting hit by vehicles along the highway each week, he says. They're also digging holes under the road.

'You know where they operate. I had a look at a couple of patches this morning.'

He pauses. And, with a glint in his eye, continues.

'They are good eating too, the wombats. It's white meat, nice light meat,' Oolie says. 'I've had corned wombat, or barbecued wombat or roasted wombat. It's similar to pork. It's rich, you've got to be careful when you eat it though; you'll drink a lot of beer.'

11

Katanning

Location: 280 km south-east of Perth.

Population: 3687

Aired: The episode on Katanning aired on New Year's Day 2017. It was the fifth episode in the second series of *Back Roads*.

FOR YEARS, ALEP MYDIE had a gnawing feeling that something just wasn't right. Deep in his subconscious. Eating away at him. He just didn't know what it was.

Then, out of the blue, a year after his appearance on *Back Roads*, a letter turned up which gave him answers to questions he'd never realised he'd had. It was a letter that his grandfather had sent to the Australian government. A single page, in fading black ink. In broken English, Bytol bin Zanlay had pleaded for help:

'What do you think sir?' he wrote. 'If Tuan John not like me and Home Islands, can I alive sir? Please keep my secret sir.'

The letter, marked 'confidential', was sent from Home Island, in the Cocos (Keeling) archipelago. It was dated 12 December 1957.

So Alep did some research. And a little bit more.

'My grandfather never told me the story,' he says. 'In my life, all these years, there's been emptiness for a reason.'

The Cocos (Keeling) Islands are made up of 27 small coral islands, due west of Darwin and about 2800 kilometres north-west of Perth. The nearest neighbour is Christmas Island, 900 kilometres away.

Alep was born on Christmas Island. Before that, his family had been living on the Cocos (Keeling) Islands but had left just before he was born. But he didn't know why.

And when he was old enough to ask questions, he'd been too focused on integrating into his new community, his new life, on mainland Australia, in Katanning, a dry and dusty service town in Western Australia's Great Southern Region, about three hours drive south-east of Perth.

Alep's family had packed up and moved to Katanning in 1974 with a handful of other families from Christmas Island to work at a new abattoir that was hiring halal slaughtermen. Their arrival would eventually change the face of Katanning. They were ethnic Malay, and practising Muslims. Alep was 15 and the eldest of four siblings.

The journey to the Western Australian mainland had taken a week in a ship laden with silver phosphate cargo, with a separate compartment for passengers. And then they had arrived. There was black-and-white television. And an outdoor toilet to get used to. It was all new to Alep and his family.

All the families helped each other. They shared a house – one family to a room – until they got settled. 'We really started from scratch,' he says. 'We were allowed to bring some of the furniture from the island, to bring it on the boat. That's what I remember.'

Back on Christmas Island, he'd grown up hearing clues about the past.

'I remember on the island, there was a lack of education facilities. My mother would tell me it was still better than Cocos Island,' Alep says.

Alep recalls feeling surprised, and delighted, when he was allowed to play with the white children at his new school in Katanning. On Christmas Island, that had been frowned on.

'We were segregated,' he says of his Christmas Island school. 'When we first went to school [in Katanning], everybody was looking at us. You wanted to be part of them. I felt so lucky: everyone wanted to know me, and I wanted to know them.'

But there were some significant hurdles. Like language.

'The lingo – you guys speak so fast!' Alep says.

He quickly learned to adapt – and thrive – in the small town where he looked and sounded different from everyone. He loved toasted cheese sandwiches from the school canteen – and he learned to love Vegemite. He refused to be excluded from anything.

'There's a lot of good people out there. And how we fit in is important. How we fit in. Not them fitting in with us.'

Back in 1974, Katanning was nothing like the bustling centre it is today.

'A ghost town,' Alep says. 'Not what you see now. Just a small town. But there was employment here because of the meatworks. That's what we came here for.'

It was slow. And quiet, Alep says. And homogenous. But he refused to be upset by casual racism, such as name-calling. He chose to see them as nicknames. And their sources as possible friends.

'When we first arrived, people wondered "where did these people come from?",' he says. 'We were called "chocca boys", or "samboy", because of our dark skin. Gradually, we learned the lingo; we learned the language. We never shied away from anything, and we learned along the way. We tripped and fell and then we learned, and in the end, at the end of the day, we know who we are.'

Katanning has had huge success as a cultural melting pot. When *Back Roads* filmed with Alep in 2016, there were migrants from 42 different nationalities living in the town of 3800. One in ten is Muslim.

Back at school though, in the beginning, Alep just wanted to fit in. He joined in everything with zest. Including at the local Baptist church.

'Three of us, we went to the camp. We went to church. We sang. I remember on weekends we'd bring curry puffs to the church and we'd all eat together.'

He wanted to learn as much as possible. About everything.

The first wave of migration by the Christmas Islanders made it easier for subsequent new immigrants to settle in Katanning.

Migrants like Zee Sultani and her family. When *Back Roads* met Zee in 2016, she was the Shire of Katanning's busy community and youth development officer, and pulling together the town's Harmony Day festivities.

She'd arrived in Katanning more than a decade earlier, as a wide-eyed and uneducated ten-year-old refugee from Afghanistan. But she still remembers touching down at Perth Airport vividly.

'It was magical,' she says. 'Like a fairy tale. Like Alice in Wonderland. It was just incredible. I will never forget that night.

'It took us years to get used to the culture, to get used to the environment, the weather. It's a huge culture shock. I think because of the Malay community being here for that long, they did all the hard work of coming and being the odd ones out and then adjusting, and getting involved in the community.'

One of the most significant things the growing Malay Muslim population of Katanning did all those years ago was build a mosque. The light-orange brick building adorned with silver minarets opened in 1980 after years of fundraising through small donations. Bit by bit, the community got closer to their goal.

'We were like nomads, going to different buildings and renting them, especially for Ramadan,' Alep remembers.

They conducted Friday prayers in the RSL hall, even in an old winery full of pigeons, until some crown land came up for sale. Alep was a teenager and the secretary of the Katanning Islamic Community at the time.

'We started to raise funds, selling curry puffs, anything we could sell we would sell, to raise funds for the mosque. Any friends that understood us, helped us – plumbers, electricians. A lot of people helped us. Looking back to see and to hear how hard it is to build a mosque 30, 40 years [on], how grateful we are.'

The mosque is now firmly established as part of the Katanning community, and regularly sponsors different sports teams in town, like cricket, soccer, basketball and netball. Even so, Alep worries about uncertainty created by the global wave of anti-Islamic sentiment.

'Katanning is really, really special. It's like a magical place, where people accept you. We know how lucky we are.'

These days Alep is Katanning's imam, its Islamic spiritual leader. He also runs a local coffee shop, the Daily Grind. And he's on the shire council. He's always held strong beliefs about tolerance, justice and freedom. And he's a natural leader. He's raised his four children here, and now has five grandchildren.

'I don't want to confine myself as the imam of the mosque and that's it, full stop,' he says. 'I would be the only imam that sits on the council, as a businessman, as a husband, a father. I just want to be a happy person. If I can make someone happy, that's rewarding for me. A smile. It's something that I can contribute to the community. I don't confine myself to the mosque every day, day in, day out. No. It would be boring.'

Alep isn't your typical imam, if there is such a thing. For starters, he's an avid fan of the US television show *Game of*

Thrones. During the AFL season he's likely to be seen in the navy and gold of his beloved West Coast Eagles as he leads the service at the mosque.

'Even my grandchildren have been brought up to be Eagles or Dockers supporters,' he says.

'Everybody knows if the Eagles win – but vice versa, if another team wins and we lose, the Eagles supporters keep quiet about it; not a word.'

The families were soccer fans when they first arrived in Australia, but they were soon converted. Everyone was a West Coast Eagles fan in the early days, but when the Freemantle Dockers came on the scene in 1994 it split the family.

'We became enemies within ourselves. My mother and some of my brothers went Eagles. My father and wife went to the Dockers.

'It changed our life. Who we are. It doesn't matter what you look like, what colour you are, if you start to wear your club shirt, people respect you.

'Unless you are a Magpie.'

It's now a year after the *Back Roads* episode on Katanning aired. Alep has expanded his coffee shop over two shopfronts. It's comfortable and inviting, full of lounges and nooks and crannies.

'If only the moon and the trees can speak to you, they'd tell you I'm so blessed,' he says.

After the show aired, some people had driven all the way from Queensland to try his curry puffs. He's doing a roaring trade. Sometimes he sells more than a hundred in a day.

'I can't keep up with it,' he says. 'I'm buying them from my mother now.'

Significantly, after the show, an academic reached out to Alep. While researching the history of the Cocos Islands he'd come across the letter Alep's grandfather had sent all those years ago, and forwarded it to him. It was shocking to Alep.

'It's so sad how my grandfather wrote this letter, asking for help,' he says.

The letter came amid a brewing dispute on the Cocos (Keeling) Islands. The family had lived on the islands for generations. The islands were uninhabited until they were settled, first by British trader Alexander Hare in 1826, and soon after by John Clunies-Ross, a Scottish seaman. Both men brought their own entourages, many of whom were originally from Indonesia. They were the island's first workforce and became known as Cocos Malays. Their numbers would be boosted years later with imported workers.

John Clunies-Ross was the first of five so-called 'Kings of the Cocos' in the family dynasty that would rule over the islands for 128 years, until the Australian government bought it out in the 1970s. During that time, the family had built a thriving copra trade, expanded the coconut tree plantations, brought in specialised machinery to process the nuts, and built workshops.

When Alep's family was living there, the Cocos Malays were born into the labour force. They were paid in Cocos Rupees, a currency only able to be used at the expensive general store, run by the island's bosses. It was the way it had been for years. And nobody challenged it.

Sheep on a hill in the picturesque town of Yackandandah, north-east Victoria. (Colin Jones)

Scaredy Cat star and much loved character around Yackandandah Moira Dale with her mother, Rebecca McGowan. Moira is still acting in local productions. (Karen Michelmore)

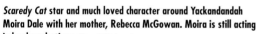

Di Reeves with one of her many outfits at her home in Violet Town. Since coming out as a transgender woman in her sixties she hasn't looked back, and is making up for all the time she's missed dressing up in the clothes she loves. (Karen Michelmore)

Birchip baker Kevin Sharp making his famous vanilla slice. Now for the thick, luscious icing. Kevin — three times national champion — has honed the craft to a fine art. (Karen Michelmore)

The view from Mount Arapiles near Natimuk, Victoria. Rock climbers from around the world gather at this massive rock structure rising out of the western plains. (Karen Michelmore)

Rock climber Louise Shepherd in her garden at Natimuk. Louise first fell under the spell of Mount Arapiles and climbing in the 1970s. (Karen Michelmore)

Gurjit Sondhu, with her black Angus beef cattle on her farm Jullundur near Harrow, western Victoria. She's been in Harrow 42 years now, and despite the pain of the past couple of years, wouldn't want to be anywhere else. (Karen Michelmore)

Ian Friend found out by chance he was a descendant of Charles Lawrence, the cricketer who captained the first Aboriginal XI on its tour of England 150 year ago. He was going through some old family boxes when he discovered many treasures, including this fob watch, from Australia's first international sporting tour. (Karen Michelmore)

Australia's Aboriginal XI cricket team beside the Members' Pavilion at the Melbourne Cricket Ground in February 1867. They'd already played a run of cricket matches when the photo was taken. It was the start of a remarkable chapter in Australia's sporting and social history. (From the collection of the Melbourne Cricket Club)

Sunrise in Mundulla, a historic township surrounded by rich agricultural country in South Australia, away from the main highways and close to the Victorian border. Not much has changed here for decades, says one of the town's stalwarts, Vida Maney. (Colin Jones)

Marie Williams is proud of her heritage. She grew up in Marree and is a descendant of one of Australia's most famous cameleers, BJ the Faithful, Bejah Dervish. The cameleers forged new paths across the remote inland, trekking thousands of kilometres with chains of camels, some 70 beasts long and carrying goods weighing several hundred kilograms. (Karen Michelmore)

Craig 'Oolie' Stinear at work in his 'office'. He's caretaker of the 620km stretch of Highway One, which traverses the length of South Australia's Great Australian Bight. (Karen Michelmore)

Presenter Heather Ewart with Burundi kids after filming with their families singing and dancing in a Katanning church hall in Western Australia. They've settled here as refugees from Africa. (Wendy Thorn)

Katanning Imam and coffee shop owner Alep Mydie outside the mosque in his beloved West Coast Eagles regalia. When *Back Roads* filmed with Alep in 2016, there were migrants from 42 different nationalities living in the town of 3,800. One in 10 are Muslim. (Wendy Thorn)

The two Heathers – Heather Jones and Heather Ewart – decked out in pink and ready to hit the road in the Pilbara. Heather runs her own successful road train business and road safety project, the Pilbara Heavy Haulage Girls, and is about to give the other Heather a driving lesson. She confides that she thinks women drive better than men. (Lou Turley)

A boab tree at sunset in Derby, in Western Australia's north. Derby was one of the first towns *Back Roads* filmed in 2015, and it remains one of the most beautiful places we've visited. (Karen Michelmore)

Kids at Mowanjum community try out the *Back Roads* camera equipment. The community is near Derby, in Western Australia's north and the children are being painted up in readiness for the Boab Mardi Gras parade in the afternoon. (Karen Michelmore)

Outgoing Boab Quest winner Trent Ozies on a float with the new finalists vying for the crown. Trent is still coming to terms with giving up his tiara but thrilled he was the first male to win the community pageant, named after the distinctive bulbous trees that dot the landscape. (Karen Michelmore)

Pine Creek veteran Eddie Ah Toy beside the town's Chinese pig oven. It's one of the few relics left from the gold rush era and Eddie and his family are the last Chinese residents in Pine Creek. (Karen Michelmore)

Elsie Seriat with Rob de Castella after she completed the New York Marathon in 2014. She finished with jelly legs, and a very respectable time of 4 hours and 36 minutes.
(Photo courtesy of the Indigenous Marathon Project)

Elsie at home in Canberra, where she moved after *Back Roads* visited her in 2016. She's working for the Indigenous Marathon Project, supporting all the previous graduates around the country to help them realise their post-marathon dreams.
(Karen Michelmore)

Presenter Heather Ewart with hairdressing team Lyn Westbury and Fil Stewart checking out the local wildlife in the main street of Normanton near the end of a nine-day road trip. These extraordinary women have travelled thousands of kilometres four times a year to give clients in remote communities a new hairdo, some pampering and a sympathetic ear.

At Winton in outback Queensland the *Back Roads* team came across former Governor General Quentin Bryce, patron of the Australian Age of Dinosaurs. She grew up in western Queensland and is passionate about the area. She told presenter Heather Ewart she wanted to pass on that love and understanding to the next generation of Australians by encouraging them to visit. (Brigid Donovan)

Full moon rising near Middleton, western Queensland (Brigid Donovan)

Winton sheep farmer turned fossil hunter David Elliott. Over the past 18 years, David, his wife Judy and an assortment of dedicated volunteers and staff have gradually uncovered the world's largest collection of Australian dinosaur fossils in David's backyard and on neighbouring properties.
(Ron Ekkel)

The Middleton Hotel. It's pretty close to the middle of nowhere. Plenty of cold beer here but travellers should not expect any luxury accommodation. (Brigid Donovan)

Presenter Heather Ewart and *Back Roads* executive producer Brigid Donovan kicking off our first series in 2015 with Middleton Hotel publican Lester Cain. This former camel trainer and tough man of the bush is renowned for never wearing shoes while serving a beer. (Ron Ekkel)

Another early start for the *Back Roads* team. It's a typical autumn morning in the high country near Corryong, Victoria, the home of the very popular Man from Snowy River Festival. (Brigid Donovan)

Cattle property owner and skilled horsewoman Joan Sinclair, still riding in her eighties. She grew up taking cattle to the high country with her father, and it's always been home. What's more, she reckons her horses are less trouble than men. (Karen Michelmore)

Former miner turned tour guide Anthony Coulsen shows Heather Ewart his treasured world heritage-listed forests just out of Queenstown, western Tasmania, over a cup of excellent billy tea brewed with local sassafras leaves.

Champion giant pumpkin grower Shane Nevitt shares his tips for success near Dunalley in Tasmania with Heather Ewart. One secret is to play music to them and every pumpkin has a name. This one is 'The Terminator'. It's a very serious business. (David Hudspeth)

The *Back Roads* crew with their 'Derby socks', filming in the squelchy mud flats at Derby, in Western Australia – cameraman Ron Ekkel, presenter Heather Ewart, producer Karen Michelmore and sound engineer John Peterson. You're up to your knees before you know it, a challenge for any camera crew. (Ron Ekkel)

Until Alep's grandfather became headman of the islands in 1957. Bytol bin Zanlay was young, educated and religious.

It was a time of change on the islands. The first and second world wars had begun to open the isolated islanders up to the world around them.

By 1955 Britain had transferred responsibility for the islands to Australia. An administrator was installed on West Island. But the family still ruled. By that stage, the fifth Clunies-Ross 'king', also called John, was in charge. The islanders, living on Home Island, relied on the family for supplies through the store. Copra prices were falling, so the islanders were asked to volunteer to work an extra two or three hours each day. Unpaid.

By November, the store supplies were also drying up. They were running out of sugar, coffee and chillies. Bytol bin Zanlay raised concerns but was told they must wait for a scheduled supply ship to arrive. He wanted to seek supplies from the Australians on West Island. Or source them themselves. But those requests were also rejected.

So a group of islanders took the initiative and sailed to meet the Australian representatives on nearby West Island. It was the first time the islanders had sought help from an external party. They were met with some sympathy.

The power held by the family for more than a century was eroding. John Clunies-Ross gave the islanders an ultimatum: they could follow him, follow the Australian government or run Cocos themselves.

Alep's grandfather was describing that choice in the letter he sent to the Australian government. Many families wanted to leave the island, including Alep's. Bytol told the Australian government he needed to leave – he was forbidden from going to other islands to sell goods or exchange and barter.

'If it is like that forever and ever, I would not be able to make friends outside or learn anything from outside, or get books from the outside world,' he explained. 'If I have a conversation in meeting people and bartering things, that will lead to improvement. I want my children to become more clever and more learned.'

On 7 June 1958, several families, including Bytol and his family – son Mydie and Alep's mother, pregnant with him – left for Christmas Island and a better life. Christmas Island officially became an Australian territory a few months later.

Alep is proud of his grandfather, for doing his best for his family and forging a new future, and for standing up and speaking out. And for understanding the importance of mixing harmoniously with people from different backgrounds. He shares these traits with his grandfather. It's an attitude Alep adopted early, first as he made Katanning home as a teenager, and later as he grew into a leader in the community.

He says finding out this piece of his family history has impacted him, profoundly.

'It is who I am. I've found out what I am doing now is for a reason. I don't know the reason why it happened, but with that history, now I can tell you who I am.'

12

Karratha

Location: 1523 km north of Perth in the Pilbara region of Western Australia.

Population: 21,473

Aired: This episode aired on Monday 22 January 2018. It was the eighth episode in the third series.

IT WASN'T UNTIL ONE of her trucking bosses hurled a sandwich at her that Heather Jones' decades-long love affair with Australia's heavy haulage industry truly began. It's a passion which has never faded, despite the ups and downs, near-misses, near-bankruptcy, threats and a frustrating, gear-crunchingly slow shift in the industry's macho culture.

Ask Heather today about the industry that tried to lock her and other women out, she'll tell you it's all about the camaraderie with those very same blokes.

'It sort of sucks you in,' she says. 'I know there's a corny saying, when diesel gets in your veins you can never leave it, but there's something about the industry and the mateship as well.'

Sitting up high in her bright-pink, 700-horsepower, 53-metre-long road train. Hurtling down an empty highway, surrounded by wide, open skies and red-rock, spinifex-clad hills. It's where she feels at home. Her long dark hair is pulled into a ponytail and bright-pink high-vis shirts, the same hue as her mammoth vehicles. Surrounded by static on the two-way, as friends drop in and out of range. With a heavy load on three trailers out back, and a set destination hundreds and hundreds of kilometres into the future. Driving one of the biggest road trucks in the world. There's really nothing quite like the feeling behind the wheel of one.

'I think every day is a fresh day. It doesn't matter what the day before brought to you,' she says. 'The sunrises and the fresh air and the birds, and the things that we see and we experience. It's just a new start to another day, and it's the best time of the day. Out on the highways it's just lovely. I love the freedom on the highway.'

Every single day is different.

She'll tell you about how tiny the trucking industry really is – and how quickly news travels. How she'll start heading out of one town, only to receive a call from a friend 1000 kilometres away saying that they've heard she's heading south; would she like to catch up for dinner?

It's not always wanted attention, mind you. Occasionally, when nature calls, Heather may be hiding off the highway in the spinifex bushes, wearing her bright-pink uniform, her bright-pink truck parked nearby.

'They can't miss you,' she says. 'If they see my truck, you'll hear them gearing down and gearing down and gearing down and you think, oh, please don't stop, I'm just going to the toilet; please don't stop, please don't stop. And they stop, and they say, oi, are you all right? And so, you know, so that's, that's the couple of funny things that happen.

'We all try and pull up in a truck bay where you know somebody, so if something does happen, then you've always got a buddy there to help you out.'

She also loves the freedom the income the occupation provides.

'You know, you can earn up to $100,000 or more driving a truck,' she says. 'And whether you're a male or a female, once you've got that load on the back of your trailer, then you become your own boss. You really can do anything.'

Being a female does matter, though, out here. Or it did, anyway. Back when Heather first started driving trucks in the 1990s, opportunities for women to gain entry in the male-dominated world were rare. Impossible even. Heather, or Jonesy as she's known, is full of stories of women who applied for jobs for ten years without success. One woman offered up 3500 separate applications without gaining an interview, before she met Heather.

But slowly there's been a shift. Female drivers, these days, are celebrated. And some of that at least is down to Heather. But it hasn't been easy.

'We will never change the old truck drivers; they actually have to die out,' she says candidly. 'We have been targeted because we are making change. And these people don't want to change. We've had sand put in fuel tanks and that sort of thing.'

As well as helping bring in more female drivers, Heather has continually pushed for improvements to training and road safety. When she first started driving trucks, drivers were simply thrown into the job.

'This was the initiation: here's the keys, jump in that truck, hook up to that trailer, go down and get a load of fertiliser and head up to the farm 600 kilometres away,' she says.

'So, I sort of got a little bit concerned being a female, because we like to know all the ins and outs and we're probably a bit more genetically safety-programmed, you know, as mothers and carers and nurturers.'

Which brings us back to the flying sandwich incident of 2004. She was working for a transport company in Perth. The lack of training and professionalism bothered her. So when the boss told her he had sent the latest female recruit off on a 'training exercise' by herself, down a hill in a large old truck with an 18-speed Roadranger gearbox, with only an automatic driver's licence, she'd had enough. She quit on the spot.

'I'm thinking: we are all going to jail,' she says. 'She's going to kill someone. So I said, I quit. I quit. He threw his sandwich at me and said I was a bloody selfish woman. I was selfish because I'd quit.'

She laughs at the memory. 'So I went home and I said to my sister, I quit today. I've got no idea what I'm going to do, but I quit. I can no longer be part of no training. I can't be part of just putting bums in seats.

'She said, well, you know how to fix it, don't you? Buy your own trucks. Start your own business.'

At the time, it was beyond Heather's comprehension, such was the huge cost of establishing a trucking business. But the beginning of an idea was forming.

No bank would help her, despite the fact she owned her own home. Eventually, a financial broker got her the money within a couple of weeks. She bought her first truck and started Success Transport. That was 14 years ago.

With her female-run company – all her daughters are involved – she became known as someone who would give new starters a go.

'In our company I never, ever, ever had to advertise for a driver. I always had a waiting list of drivers wanting to come and drive for us. And I treat everyone like my family too.'

A lack of training, an endemic 'boys' club' attitude and an ageing workforce was eating away at the industry, leading to a serious decline in numbers of available drivers. The government was examining a proposal to bring in overseas drivers on 457 foreign worker visas because there weren't enough drivers in Australia. There was a suggestion that young men weren't interested in the industry. And women didn't drive trucks.

It was enough to spur Heather into action. She and other female truck drivers formed an organisation called Pilbara Heavy Haulage Girls.

'We sort of thought, obviously we aren't visible enough and there were a lot of women from our experience that want to drive trucks, and a lot of young guys, but the missing link was the training or the work experience that they could actually do so that then they could qualify for the jobs that were advertised.'

To become more visible, they all wore pink work shirts.

'Normally they come to us with their licence and then we put them in the truck for 160 hours, in a real, live work environment, which is where the new driver gets their three to four weeks work experience up,' she says.

'Because when you get your licence, you're licensed to steer the cab part of the truck and maybe hook up a trailer, but all the load restraint, tyre changing, permit reading, different trailer configurations, oversize load requirements and so much more is just not taught to you.'

After they formed Pilbara Heavy Haulage Girls they did a few radio interviews. More and more people started contacting the organisation, asking to be trained. So Heather started writing to companies to see if any of them would help with funding.

'We were looking for about $20,000 so we could just do a 12-month rental on a training facility so that we could run our trucks and train these few people,' she says. 'We sent out 220 sponsorship packages and we had one reply, and it wasn't $20,000. It was Volvo Group Australia offering us 12 months with two brand-new trucks to use in the training we were doing. I nearly dropped dead!'

These days the team trains about 15 people a year in the trucks. Almost all have gained employment, most within a couple of weeks of graduating.

Even so, Heather prefers being out on the highways driving the trucks. 'If I have the opportunity to head out by myself, it's my sanity time,' she says.

She also uses the time to reflect on some of the other problems in the industry: rest areas, healthy food at service stations. It all leads back to safety.

'If you eat pies, pasties, sausage rolls and wash it down with a can of Coke, that contributes significantly to fatigue and to [poor] driver health', she says. 'If you've got healthy food: boiled eggs, carrot sticks, celery sticks, little beetroot that you can just pick and eat when you're driving, it helps you stay alert and healthy. A container of nuts and sultanas is good to have as well.'

Today she's off to Newman, a mining town in the eastern reaches of the Pilbara, to deliver accommodation units to a mine site. It's a seven-hour drive.

'Just down the road,' she says.

It's one of her favourite spots.

'When we hit the Newman–Hedland road, there are a lot of quad road trains passing us every one to two minutes with four trailers swinging behind each one, and they would have to be some of the most polite truck drivers in Australia,' she says. 'Come up behind them and they'll call you up on the two-way radio and they'll say, "Copy in the Volvo behind TK123, you're good to come around now". They're amazing. Really great.'

She passes a dead cow by the side of the road, on its back with its legs in the air. There's a lot of stock roaming freely beside the road, let alone wildlife: sheep, cattle, goats, emus, kangaroos, brumbies. They even have to dodge camels on the northern highways.

Another potential hazard is the tourists: 'I don't think they'd like me to put them in the "hazard" category but, you need to put them in the "be aware" category, anyhow,' she says.

She's had a few near-misses.

'We often have something happen every single day,' she says. 'You've got to drive defensively for others in your workplace. Often you need to watch what the car driver is doing in front of you or travelling towards you, then try to predict what they are going to do, as so often they will just pull off the road with no indication or just stop dead in front of you.

'I had 150-tonne on a road train once and I had a grey nomad just stop dead in front of me because they saw an eagle they wanted to take a photo of, and I don't know whether it was a hazard for them or for me, but I must have missed them by the skin of my teeth,' she says.

'I've had international tourists driving on the wrong side of the road, heading towards me, and I've had to take my road train off the road to save their life.'

It's no wonder safety is of vital importance to Heather. One of her earliest memories from childhood is the aftermath of an accident in which she and her mother, Connie, were both seriously injured. She was just two.

Her mother was behind the wheel of the white Volkswagen Beetle, heading back along the highway to their home in

Harvey, south of Perth, when a drink driver came over the hill, headed straight for the car. Connie swerved to avoid him and the vehicle rolled six or more times. Heather was crushed in the front passenger child car seat, her head out the window. Her mother broke several ribs on the steering wheel. Both required ongoing treatment for years afterwards, and it was a matter of frequent family discussion during Heather's childhood.

'There were regular conversations about the drink driver, and how he'd caused so much damage to our little family through his actions, but also that it could have been so much worse.'

She was brought up to be strong and independent – her father, Ron, made the girls do the same jobs as the boys in their large household. 'There were nine of us kids in the family and there was no gender-specific jobs,' she recalls. 'Seven girls, two boys. All of us girls had to lay concrete, help put up fences, fix cars, change tyres, and the boys had to cook and clean and sew buttons on their shirts.'

Years later, when Ron was working on a mine in the Pilbara, he told her about a job going. The mine manager was looking for a personal assistant and she jumped at the chance. Over time she realised how much more the iron ore dump truck drivers were being paid than the office staff. And they were hiring.

'I looked at what the earnings were for a driver of a dump truck, and I looked at what I was earning for being on call 24 hours a day and I thought, God, I could go home every weekend, sleep and earn nearly twice as much as I do now. That's how I got in. It was great.'

She'd been married in the Pilbara and had two daughters, Kirsty, four, and Chelsea, three.

'As often marriages do, mine failed so I had a new challenge and that was how to feed and educate my children by myself,' she says. 'I actually couldn't afford child care so I had really good friends who were managing a trucking company in Karratha, and they said as long the girls don't get out of the cab, Heather, you can come and work for us. So that's what we did. We drove a truck up here and down in Perth for the next seven years, with my girls in the bunk.'

She homeschooled the girls, bringing in tutors to help when they weren't on the road.

'It was a really good decision because they met more people and have seen more of the country than I think most Australians have,' she says.

It hasn't always been easy. She had to sell down after clients baulked on $2.7 million owed to her amid the global financial crisis in 2009. It never entered her mind to give up, though.

'We had to get rid of everything,' she says. 'We had two beautiful yards, 23 working trucks and trailing gear. Had to sell everything and then get back into the truck and bust my arse to pay off the debt.'

She'd invested too much of herself to give up, and hadn't finished the job she'd started. Plus she wanted to leave the business to her daughters.

'This is all they know and I'd like to be able to leave this business to them so they can change the world,' she says.

'I know that sounds corny. But if we don't effect change, no one else will.'

Driving down the highways of the north-west of Western Australia, Heather has a lot of time to think about the other things she wants to fix.

'It's a good bit of thinking time.'

13

Derby

Location: 2496 km north-east of Perth; 220 km east of Broome, on King Sound in the Kimberley.

Population: 3511

Aired: The *Back Roads* episode about Derby was one of the first filmed for the show, in July 2015. It was broadcast on 4 January 2016.

TRENT OZIES IS SOMEWHAT reluctant to remove his tiara. He's worried that when he does, it might be for the last time.

The 23-year-old is sitting in a comfortable red leather chair in his soundproof radio studio, the tiny silver crown tucked beneath his headphones. It twinkles bright against his long, jet-black hair.

There's a blue wall-hanging featuring two large dolphins on the red-brick wall behind him. And piled on the desk in front are books of jokes and riddles and freaky facts. His phone is on silent but buzzes constantly.

'Good morning!' he chirps into the microphone. 'It's your boy Trenty O here in the studios of 6DBY 97.9 FM. We've got quite a few things happening today.'

It's a big day for the outback Western Australian town of Derby, but it's a huge day for Trent. It's mid–dry season 2015 and the height of the tourist season. The town's main festival is on today. And thus it's also officially Trent's last day as winner of the Boab Quest – a community pageant named after the distinctive bulbous trees that dot the landscape. A new winner will be crowned tonight. He's stretched out his title for as long as he can.

'My last day with my crown,' he frowns. 'It's all right; I'm still the real queen of Derby. I don't care what anyone says.'

Trent's got an irrepressible, flamboyant outlook on life. Sometimes he's effervescent. Bubbling. Always fun. He loves making people laugh, and chuckles to himself effortlessly and often in his role as an on-air presenter at the Derby Media Aboriginal Corporation radio station.

No topic is off limits. He regularly pokes gentle fun at himself. Trent refuses to take the world too seriously. Unless, of course, his tiara is at stake. Obviously.

Trent started volunteering at the radio station when he was 13. About the same age he was when he came out as gay to his family and friends. It was a brave step in the outback town. No one else had spoken so publicly about their homosexuality before Trent took to the airwaves. Nor since.

It sounds counterintuitive, but Trent likes the freedom the microphone gives him. Freedom to be himself. Plus he hopes his voice helps others struggling with their own identity.

'I think it's allowed me to become a role model in a way that I can express who I am as a person,' he reflects. 'You know how you look at TV shows and there's always that token black character? That's how I feel being in a town like this – I'm the token black, gay character.

'But I take that to my advantage and I don't let it become a negative. And I think that's what makes me feel confident, feel different in a good sense, that I can be who I want to be. I don't care, and at the end of the day, if you don't like me then it's not my problem. It's yours.'

Derby is a small town, with red dirt roads off the main strip. It's surrounded on three sides by mudflats – during low tide it's a brown marsh, stretching as far as the eye can see. Sandflies roam freely. And bite.

It's a place with a unique rhythm of its own, with the highest tides in the Southern Hemisphere, occasionally rising and dropping back up to ten metres within in a single day.

Things ebb and flow here. They come and go.

Every night, though, there's one constant: the sun sets spectacularly. The sea swallows the large, glowing ball of fire. People gather around the jetty to watch and take photos, as the wide sky lights up red, then pink. And orange.

Trent loves the natural beauty of Derby. As well as the community.

'It feels like you know everybody,' he explains. 'The heart of this town is the fact that everyone says hello. No one is going to snob you or ignore you – if you say hello to someone you're going to get a hello back, and that's a guaranteed fact.'

Trent's a member of the Kimberley's Djugan Aboriginal tribe. He was born in Broome, west of Derby, where his mother, Narelle, grew up. His father, Tony, is from Derby.

For the first eight or so years of his life, he lived with his parents and five siblings in a small bush community on a massive cattle station along the remote and wild Gibb River Road, about a day's drive from Derby.

Life was simple. And free. The kids would go to school up the road, and fish and swim in the pristine waters at Hann River, Manning Gorge or Abcock Gorge on the weekends.

'It was a good little life,' he says. 'Dad used to help muster the cattle. Some weekends if I was lucky enough I'd get to go with him on what they'd called a bull buggy.

'It's like an old buggy-type car. There's no windscreen. They had two tyres on the front. And roll bars. So they used to knock the cattle over with the tyres and you'd get a group of young men on the bull buggy and they'd have to tie the back legs and all of that stuff.'

The family lived in the old nurses' quarters on the homestead, in a three-bedroom house with an open-plan lounge and kitchen. And a large mango tree outside next door.

'There was one Brahman bull that liked to eat the mangoes when they dropped, so that was its home,' he says. 'He used to try and chase us when we used to run to school on a Monday morning.'

But Trent's most enduring memory is the Friday night family dinners. Sitting on a sheet with his brother and four sisters on the lounge room floor. Giggling. Watching telly. And eating takeaway Chinese food collected from Derby, hundreds of kilometres away, by the helicopter that mustered the cattle.

'Mum would ring up and make an order on a Thursday night and Butch, the helicopter pilot, would fly in with the cheque, pick up the Chinese on the Thursday night, put it in his fridge and then he'd fly out on the Friday to help muster over the weekend,' he says.

Trent was born on New Year's Eve, a situation he describes as both a 'gift and a curse'.

'As a child it wasn't very nice. My birthday's after Christmas – everyone's broke! I didn't get no birthday presents. If I was lucky enough to get $20 and a card, I was grateful for that.'

But now he's grown up he loves it.

'It's a gift because as we all know New Year's Eve is a time for celebration. And we all love going to celebrations. For the celebrations.'

He smiles. It's clear he loves a party. And on New Year's Eve it can feel as if the whole world is wishing him a happy birthday.

He's ready to celebrate today. Even if he is giving up his title. And his Boab Quest tiara. He's preparing to hand it over to a new winner, along with the accompanying purple satin cape with white fur trim he wears over his T-shirt and shorts. But they'll get one more outing first – albeit in 30-degree heat – when Trent takes his seat on a float with the incoming Quest finalists in the Derby Mardi Gras parade this afternoon.

'I am a delicate soul and a beautiful flower that is going to shrivel and wither in the heat,' he tells a friend.

The floats are made up of trucks, utes and cars, dressed up with joyful balloons and handmade signs, and filled with excited children. One long procession will roll down the wide main street, lined with supportive onlookers mingled among the boab trees, and onwards to the oval, where carnival rides and dagwood dogs will sit comfortably with live music onstage, before the traditional handing-on of the Boab crown.

Trent's in the first float. It's decorated with pot plants and a large white sheet of cardboard handwritten with '2015 BOAB QUEST ENTRANTS'. He'll sit tall on a leather chair on the vehicle's tray with the new contenders and wave with a broad smile. Like a king.

Different songs blast from each vehicle, filled with face-painted children waving as they crawl past Derby Memorial Swimming Pool. Children dressed in clown wigs grin from the back of one balloon-clad truck, followed by a new group dressed as nurses in red capes and white hats.

Later, on stage, hours after sunset, Trent will proudly hand over the cloak and tiara to a new winner, with a warm embrace. And a warning.

'You look after my baby, now. I've had this thing for 12 months. Haven't lost it yet,' he grins. 'Now remember: we are family. I love you. I'm going to give you my tiara but I want to borrow it on weekends. Okay?'

It used to be called the Boab Queen competition, until Trent won it a year ago. He was the first bloke in its 54-year history to do so.

Trent raised $7500 for his beloved radio station by hosting a series of events around the town.

'I'm still so grateful,' he says. 'I feel so blessed, being a male in a female competition. They opened it up to males and I won it.

'It was all about breaking barriers for me. And building more self-confidence. I am gay. Being from a small town, some people have a lot of negative experiences with that. But I think because I grew up there as a young child, everyone knew who I was. My mum and dad figured it out before I could really say it. I think a lot of people felt that way as I was growing up.'

Winning the Boab Quest gave Trent greater insight into the role he's played in the community so far. He talks about himself on radio, in part so others don't feel they are alone.

'A lot of people have come up and spoken to me one on one and said, you know, we appreciate what you've done,' he says. 'You've been a role model for us in that sense. If I've helped someone understand themselves and who they are as a person, you know, it's a great feeling to know I can be that person who has helped someone.'

Yet there's a sadness underlying the community, following a spate of suicides in recent years.

'Derby is a beautiful town. It's got beautiful people. But it's like a wave. You've got your ups and you've got your downs. They weren't just numbers. They weren't statistics. These are friends; these are family members; these are people that I've grown up with, that I went to school with. These are kids that I played in the playground with. It's a personal thing for me. It does hit a strong chord in my heart.

'I mean, I've been there once or twice in my life and that was due to drugs or alcohol, so I know that there's got to be something else that's making these young people want to harm themselves,' he says.

'I'm lucky I have a very supportive family and I have a strong network of friends and I decided that I wanted a better me and it's sad that some of my school friends, some of my family members, don't feel like they have that opportunity.'

Family is everything to Trent. And it's become even more important in recent years.

It's now 2018. Three years after *Back Roads* came to town. Trent moved away, but has come back home. He's had worsening health problems. His uric acid levels are spiking, crazily. It's caused gout, a form of inflammatory arthritis causing painful swelling in Trent's joints. Despite chronic pain, his positivity is resolute.

'It's affected my social life, my friends and my family. I think at the end of the day if you have a mindset that is negative then you are just going to feel down in the dumps. But if you make an effort to stay positive then things still look bright.

'I still have dreams. I still have aspirations that I want to achieve. And I know I'm going to do them one day. It might not be today or tomorrow but in a month's time, maybe in six months, maybe a couple of years. If that's how long it takes then that's how long I'm going to give it.'

The pain started just after *Back Roads* wound up filming. It's gotten worse.

'The pain can be quite severe. Anything on an affected joint, something as light as even a sheet, can feel like a ton of bricks. It's a very sharp pain. It's very sensitive to touch, to movement. It's not very nice.'

The pain got so bad, and disruptive, he had to quit his job at the radio station. For the past couple of years he's been flying back and forth to Perth for answers. It's a ten-hour round trip by car and plane.

'Doctors thought I had rheumatoid arthritis so I went to see a lot of different specialists. I think all up I must have done maybe 18 or 19 trips to Perth from the Kimberley. What frustrated me the most was I wanted to work, I wanted to be in the workforce and contribute to my community how I've always done, and the hardest part was not being able to do that,' he says.

'After I put my resignation in, having good days going down town and seeing people who used to listen to my show. They've told me that they miss me on the radio, things like that. That really frustrated me that I couldn't provide them with some form of happiness for one time throughout their day. So that was the hardest part for me. Not only that but when I did have my major flare-ups I felt like a burden on my family.

'My younger brother's got a mental delay; even though he is 23 now, he's got the mental ability of maybe a 12-year-old. So he knows I'm in pain; he doesn't know what's happening but he's compassionate. He takes time out of his day to help me get out of bed, go to the bathroom, to get meals, so being an older sibling you don't want to have that feeling of burden on a younger sibling.

'I've grown to live with it now. I know it's serious, but I don't take it seriously. I believe that if I did take it seriously I'd be a very "hate-the-world", nasty type of person, you know. It would be: Why me? Why did this have to happen to me? What did I do to anybody. Like, that type of mentality.

'And it's just toxic and you can't live life like that. I'm not taking back from anybody who wants to live their life that way; if it works for them, it works for them. But it definitely does not work for me.'

He's looking at pursuing a different career now. When he can. He's thinking of going into real estate.

'I love the media, don't get me wrong. I love being on air, making people laugh. Gosh, there's so many different aspects to that. Hearing people's stories, finding out their lives and the struggles they've had to go through to get to where they've been.'

At 26, he's been doing it for more than half his life, though.

'I want to try something new. I want to see if I can take my creativeness somewhere else,' he says.

'My dad has always been the type of person that if you can't change the outcome then don't stress about it,' he reflects. 'Change what you can change. And just do your best. So Dad's instilled that in us kids from a very young age. Mum as well. She's always told us, do the best you can in life, and if you can't be the best then be your best.'

Some things have changed a lot, but Trent's outlook hasn't.

Giving up the tiara still hurts too.

'Let's not go there,' he laughs.

14

Pine Creek

Location: 225 km south-east of Darwin, in the Northern Territory.

Population: 328

Aired: Pine Creek was the seventh episode in the third series of *Back Roads*. It first aired on Monday 15 January 2018.

EDDIE CHEONG AH TOY can't wipe the grin off his face.

'Welcome to Pine Creek! It's great to see you've all come down again.'

He's in his element as he holds court, arms outstretched, in his large, tinder-dry backyard in Pine Creek. Two or three vehicle-loads of young men, women and children who've just driven in jump out and begin unloading large plastic bags. They're all wearing matching yellow T-shirts and black pants with a red waistband. Except Eddie. He's dressed in a blue and pink T-shirt tucked neatly into his regular brown shorts. With his usual wide brown hat. His delight is genuine as he fusses around his visitors.

'Hi, Uncle Eddie,' a small boy in a yellow shirt says.

'Hello. Welcome!' A hug is next.

A young man and woman carefully unzip a large red bag to reveal the ornate yellow head of a Chinese lion. The Chung Wah Society's lion dance troupe has driven down in convoy from Darwin, about two and a half hours to the north. They left early, when the weather was still temperate.

It's blazing hot now.

In about half an hour, to the sounds of clanging cymbals and the beat of a large round black drum, four Chinese lions – made up of two performers apiece under each vibrant, glittering cloak – will saunter and wiggle their way playfully down the slopes of a hill in Pine Creek's Miners' Park. They'll jiggle past the rusted antique mining equipment and the lone boab tree at the top, downhill, right up into the faces of the onlookers who will snap away on their cameras and mobile phones, then past the trough full of water where six or seven people of various ages will look up in wry amusement as they momentarily break from their gold-panning practice.

The group has come to perform the traditional Chinese Lion Dance at the 2017 Pine Creek Gold Rush festival. It's a homage to the town's first Chinese settlers. And its mining history. It's the biggest event held in the town each year.

Gold was first discovered in Pine Creek in 1860, apparently by workers building the Overland Telegraph line from Adelaide to Darwin. The discovery sparked a gold rush, attracting thousands to the isolated outpost. Many of them were Chinese workers brought in as indentured labourers contracted to work for half the European rate of pay.

Within a decade or so, there were thought to be more than 6000 Chinese in the Northern Territory – four times the number of European settlers. The Chinese didn't just search for gold, they also helped build the North Australia Railway in searing heat, through remote wilderness from Darwin in the north, south to Katherine, then to Larrimah and finishing at Birdum. It was completed in 1889.

Eddie, 80, is the last remaining descendant of those men in Pine Creek, along with his adult daughter, Amanda, who is ambivalent about staying.

'We're the only family left in Pine Creek at the moment,' Eddie says. 'I suppose I'm used to it now – we've been the only Chinese family in town for probably 50 years.'

It's the dry season in Australia's north and while the nights are cooler, the land is thirsty. Every year, the day before the annual festival a council worker will turn on the pumps so that Pine Creek is saturated and there's water for the tourists and locals to compete in the gold-panning competition. Contestants have ten minutes to find as much of the shiny metal as they can.

Earlier, Eddie had been hard at work filling about a dozen yellow, green and orange buckets with sand from the back of a trailer and lugging them down to the creek. They'll be used in the event.

'Keeps you fit,' he smiles.

You'll often see Eddie about, mowing his lawn or otherwise energetically occupied. He's naturally industrious. He likes to keep busy.

Pine Creek is a few minutes detour off the Stuart Highway, about an hour north of Katherine. It's home to Aboriginals from the Jawoyn, Mayali and Wagiman language groups. Between April and September it's a regular stop-off for tourists to stretch their legs as they snake their way from Darwin, or to Kakadu. Or for birdwatchers keen to spot a rare hooded parrot attracted to Pine Creek's tranquillity.

Tranquil, that is, except for the large mob of shrieking fruit bats living in the mahogany trees near the old Pine Creek railway station.

'You might say they're part of the population,' Eddie says.

Pine Creek was booming when Eddie's grandfather, Jimmy Ah You, arrived in Queensland from southern China and made his way to the remote town.

'He had a team of horses, about six or eight horses, with a dray and he was carting goods up and down the railway, when they were building the Darwin to Katherine section back in 1880,' Eddie says.

The construction of the railway was an incredible feat. He says the pieces of heavy track were each around 20 foot, or six metres, long.

'Imagine in those days when there were no cranes or forklifts and things like that,' he says. 'Maybe eight or ten people would have to lift it up and place it into position. There were no gloves so they probably used sugar bags or potato sacks or something. To do it in that heat would have been quite hard work. I think they were all tough when they were building the railways.'

The men were treated poorly. Many died in the harsh conditions, and over time those who remained left to seek their fortune elsewhere. When they were mining, they lived in Pine Creek's Chinatown, a hilly area out the back of town, where they would camp and cook communally. They built a Chinese temple, or joss house.

'When you go there now you can't see a sign of anything out there at all, really,' Eddie says. 'You don't know where they all lived or how they survived out there.'

There are a few clues, though. If you scour around you might find some pieces of old porcelain. Or a speck of gold. It's a popular area with prospectors, but the ground's been gone over time and again.

The land is a rabbit warren of rocky holes where the old mines used to be. There's only one relic left from that time – a structure of stone and mortar with cladding made from termite mound mortar, hidden in long grass and scrub.

'HERITAGE SITE NO. 8', reads a notice. 'PLEASE DO NOT DAMAGE.' It's partially surrounded by the remnants of a wire fence.

'This is what they call a pig oven,' Eddie says. 'They'd suspend the pig on a rod here and then they'd cover it over and let the pig bake in here until it was roasted.'

The Chinese miners are long gone. As is the cemetery where many of them were buried.

'It was Chinese custom in those days that they would exhume the bones after a certain period and they would send them back to their homeland in China,' Eddie says. 'I believe they put them in large jars. That's how they smuggled gold out of Australia, in the bottom of the jars with the bones on top.'

There's not much left these days except Eddie's stories.

After working along the railway to Pine Creek, Eddie's grandfather moved to nearby Mount Diamond, married and opened a butcher's shop. The couple had ten children.

The family returned to Pine Creek in 1922, bringing the whole building, in pieces, with them. They started baking and selling handmade bread, using ovens made from clay sourced from the region's iconic large termite mounds. Eddie's father, Jimmy, was seven years old.

Thirteen years later, in 1935, Jimmy opened a general store in the main street, a few doors down from the bakery, and called it Ah Toy's. A large white building with a red sign on the awning and a petrol bowser out the front, it now lies silent, but for 80 years it saw much activity.

Jimmy married Lily Wong the year after setting up the shop. Eddie was the first of five siblings, arriving a year later.

He's proud that he was delivered by Clive Fenton, the Northern Territory's first flying doctor, who used to traverse the outback in a gypsy moth.

'He was a real character, apparently,' Eddie says. 'He came on the Saturday and realised my mum was close, so he stayed Saturday and delivered me on the Sunday.' Eddie's grin is infectious.

As a boy he started working in the shop, as his own children later did.

'I always helped stacking the shelves,' he says. 'In those days you got rice in bulk and you had to put them into bags, and sugar was loose and we put that in paper bags and used to tie them up with string. There was no sticky tape in those days – I remember doing that. There was no pre-packaged foods. It was all just done in bulk.'

His daughter, Amanda, remembers that as soon as she and her siblings were old enough they would put price labels on goods, and once they were tall enough, would serve on the till.

'Sometimes I actually used to have my rollerskates on and skate around, and sort of work and skate,' she smiles. 'My grandfather would get right up me and tell me don't bump into the customers, which I never did, but it was fun because the floors were concrete.'

During World War II, Darwin was evacuated because of Japanese bombing raids. Pine Creek became an important transit point for the troops.

Eddie and his family were evacuated to Adelaide.

'We came back in 1945 after the war,' Eddie says. 'Mum went inside and then she completely burst into tears because the army had occupied the area and there was nothing left in the building. So the Ah Toys had to start from scratch. It was quite hard.

'We were the first civilian store to open in the Top End.'

They rebuilt the shop, and their business. Eddie went to Darwin and completed four years of high school before returning to work in the Pine Creek store. He came back to help his father run it for just a few years.

'A few years, probably five years, but it's turned into 60 years,' he says.

The store finally closed for good in 2015 amid the mining downturn. Eddie was 78. He couldn't manage it by himself and had no one to take over.

'In [2014] we lost more than half the population of the town, so, you know, it just wasn't viable to keep going, I'm afraid. It was very tough, especially after you've been trading for 80 years and I'd been here since 20 January 1955, which was 60 years. It was a very sad time for us.'

In its day Ah Toy's sold everything from guns to groceries.

'We had a roll of saddlecloth we used to cut into the lengths that people wanted,' Eddie says. 'Did I mention the coarse salt [used] to salt the buffalo hides and the crocodile skins?'

The shop even stored uranium for a time. In the late 1950s or early 1960s, Eddie would drive drums of fuel out to a company about 100 kilometres to the east, in what is now Kakadu National Park.

'For backloading they would load us up with 16 drums of yellowcake,' he says. 'Sometimes there would be some of that yellow dust all around the edges. In those days you didn't have gloves. We used to put it on our old petrol ramp at the back there. We'd accumulate maybe three to four loads and they'd arrange for a semi to come in and take it away. But there could have been over half a million dollars' worth of uranium stuck out in the yard, with no security or nothing.'

Walking through the old shop now is like visiting a museum. It's full of empty vegetable stands and magazine racks. Eddie admits he felt a bit lost after the shop closed. But he tries to keep busy.

'When you're used to coming in and opening a shop at nine every morning and that, you get a bit lost about what do you do,' he says.

Pine Creek was still struggling when *Back Roads* visited in mid-2017.

'It's the quietest time that Pine Creek has experienced,' he says. 'I haven't seen it as slow as this before, to be honest. Pine Creek has always been a mining town. There's always been ups and downs right through Pine Creek's life. It's just one of those down periods at the moment.'

Amanda adds, 'It's pretty quiet at the moment. I'm not sure what I'm going to do with myself, whether or not I'll stay or just move up the road a bit further and then keep coming back to visit Dad.'

She's proud of her Chinese heritage.

'I've always introduced myself as, you know, as of fourth-generation Australian–Chinese heritage,' she says.

They'd both like to keep the stories of Pine Creek's Chinese history alive. If they can.

'I've been part of it for so long that it would be good to keep it on,' Eddie says. 'There's talk about whether we should turn this into a Chinese museum but I suppose that's going to take lots of organising. There's so much old stuff around already – including me. No, I'm maturing. That's the word I use. I don't say I'm old. I'm maturing.'

Eddie believes the town needs a new mine to start up to

bring things to life. His daughter thinks the town's future lies in tourism.

'But tourism only goes on for about seven months of the year during the dry season,' Eddie retorts. 'The other five months, the businesses have got to survive without much business. It's very hard for them.'

The annual Gold Rush festival is part of that. It draws tourists in to celebrate the town's rich history. The Chung Wah dancers are there every year to perform the traditional lion dance. The dance is believed to bring good luck, joy, fortune and happiness. One day, it might be the only reminder of the hardworking Chinese legacy in these parts.

'I suppose you do feel sad when something has gone and there's only bits of the remains,' Eddie says. 'But that's all part of it, isn't it – it wouldn't be history if things aren't moving on.'

15

Karumba

Location: 2155 km north-west of Brisbane, in the Gulf of Carpentaria in Queensland.

Population: 531

Aired: The *Back Roads* episode on Karumba aired on Monday 21 December 2015. It was the fourth episode in the first series.

LYNE RUSSELL HAS SEEN a few unusual sights in a lifetime of working across the vast oceans, on prawn trawlers. Like the time the net dragged the ocean floor in the Gulf of Carpentaria in the Top End of Australia, and trawled up a toilet. You see, in the first days after toilets became a health and safety requirement on trawlers they didn't get the plumbing quite right.

'A lot of them, they did this backwash thing,' she recalls. 'You'd be sitting down comfortably and you'd do your business, and then it would all wash back up. Like a big wave. One of the skippers was sitting on it one time and he had a bad case of diarrhoea. When it backwashed back up he went and got a mallet and smashed it off and threw it over the side.'

So the story goes. Sometime later, the languishing latrine was fished out of the sea by Lyne's team.

'You trawl up the odd dinghy but you don't trawl up very much,' she insists.

The vessels trawl in pretty shallow water in the Gulf, according to Lyne. Sometimes she'd be working on a trawler which would spill its nets full of sea creatures directly onto the deck, rather than into a sorting tray.

'That used to be interesting because you'd bring up a big shark or a sawfish and it would be on the deck chasing you,' she says.

It was her office, and she loved it. But not in the beginning.

Lyne is a pioneer of the trawling game. She's one of the few women in Australia to spend decades on trawling boats. For weeks or months at a time.

When *Back Roads* visited Lyne in 2015, she was 62. She's been at sea off and on for maybe 40 years. Or more. She's tanned and slender, with an undeniable strength that only decades of physical work can engender. When she wasn't on the water, you'd find her heaving boxes inside a trawler that's sailed into port to unload.

Karumba is a fishing village in the far north of Queensland, known as 'the outback by the sea'. It's the end of the road, a single road, up from Normanton. It opens out onto the Gulf of Carpentaria. It's idyllic and peaceful, but the landscape is harsh, the sun unrelenting. It's a place of extremes, where drought can turn the place to dust, only to be followed by a season of rain and flooding that will cut access to the remote point for a month or more. It's both isolation and community. It's been Lyne's home, mostly, since 1972.

Today she's lifting large white boxes of frozen prawns off one conveyor belt up to another, inside a vessel docked at the port. Box by box, she will lift 16 tons of tiger prawns onto the belt, which will roll them into the nearby factory for sorting and distribution. Her hair is tied back in a long braid down her back and she's wearing a red sun visor and black fingerless gloves. It's fast manual labour.

'There's a freedom in working really, really hard,' she says. 'When I was 16, I was picking apples. There was just me and Dad. You had to lug this great big iron ladder with you and you had a harness around you and this great big bag around your neck.

'I remember thinking, oh God, but there's a point at which you don't feel the pain. There is a point where you are so fit you can work all day and at the end of the day you just feel energised.

'It took years to get to that point. When your body is supremely fit your mind can actually go into a space, all day long. It's like your mind becomes free of your body. That's an addiction too.'

Lyne wasn't always interested in boats. There was a time, in fact, when she dreaded going to sea.

'I hated every minute of it,' she says. 'I was so frightened, I'd grit my teeth. But we were only doing three-week trips back in those days. You'd go out for three weeks, come in for two. So every time I'd think, oh God, I hate this, I hate this, I hate this, oh, the smell of prawns, the smell of diesel, oh God, I just want to vomit, oh no, I hate it, I hate it, there's got to be more to life than this. And then you'd come into port and within a week you'd be like, oh God, when are we going? There's nothing to do here. When are we going?'

Lyne and her family – parents John and Ida, two sisters and a brother – moved to Karumba in the early 1970s. She was 18. She started working in one of the processing factories with her sisters, where she met her then boyfriend, Mick. Mick was a deckhand on a prawn trawler. One day his workmate, another deckhand, was too sick to go to sea. So Mick talked the skipper, Bob, into taking Lyne onto the vessel, as a prawn sorter and cook.

The trawler was called *The Sea Fever.*

'The skipper didn't want to take me because I was very skinny and he said, "Oh, she'll just cave; she won't be able to work,"' she says. 'But because I'd spent my life with Dad fruit picking or putting up fences, seriously, I had stamina. I could just work all night and then all day and then take a watch. I just stayed on that boat for years. I just loved it.'

It was hard at first, though. Lyne was the only woman on board. She was shy back then too. There were no showers, or toilets. And only a limited supply of fresh water.

'It was horrific,' she says. 'I'm just one of those people who really need to achieve. I need to do well. I need to be seen to be a hard worker and I knew the skipper didn't really want a girl on the boat. And I was shy. I was still really shy back then.'

She'd only speak to Mick, really, to find out what she should be doing.

'Being shy, I didn't like to tell anybody that I was going to the toilet and I was too scared of getting sprung so I just got constipated,' she says. 'Eventually I told my boyfriend. He said, "I never see you go to the toilet, Lyne," and I said, "That's because I don't go." And he said, "We've got a nice big wide rail there and you can hang onto that steel post." And I said, "But I don't want to, because what if Bob walks out?" He said, "Well, just tell him." I said, "I don't like to." He said, "How long since you've been?" I said, "I haven't been this whole trip." He said, "But we've been at sea ten days!" I said, "I know. I do a quick wee." So he went in and he said, "Bob, Lyne hasn't had a shit for ten days."'

Lyne was mortified.

'Bob got on the radio phone and said, "All ships, all ships, shipping hazard, shipping hazard. Cook hasn't had a shit for ten days and she's about to go." All these voices came back and said, "Tie a light on her – we don't want to run over anything like that." But after that I lost my horror and we got to be really good friends. I loved that boat.'

It's more than that. It feels like home.

'Every boat I was ever on, it just feels like a privilege,' she says. 'Some people feel like that in the desert. You look around to that 360-degree vista and it makes you feel small but big. It's the same at sea. You just look around. And at night-time sometimes when they used to change the fuel filters or something, they'd turn the engines off, everything goes dark and there's no noise; you just hear the lapping water and you look up and there's just that dome of stars. You don't even see them in the city any more. It's just this inky-black jewelled thing up there. It's just brilliant and beautiful.'

She says she was lucky: she always worked with fairly nice people. Well, except for the odd one or two.

'You know, there's always someone to talk to at two o'clock in the morning. Someone will be on watch. I used to go out to sea and people used to be suspicious. It used to be, oh God, there's a girl on the boat. But when you've gone out there and then they realise you work hard and when you've done your work you go and give them a hand, it changes – and then you get that respect and then you start getting addicted to getting the respect from really tough men who don't particularly like women.

'It's a challenge. You go, "You'll respect me, you bastard," and after a while they do. And then they turn really soft and then when you get older you are sort of like their mother confessor. They will tell you all their problems.'

Because of the lifetime of physical activity, Lyne's in remarkable health. Except for her eyes.

'I've got macular degeneration. I've had it for about four years,' she says. 'It's sort of to a point now where I can't read, and I don't really drive my car that much. But I've got to go and have eye surgery next week. I've got pterygiums on my eyes as well. A non-malignant growth you get on your eye, usually caused by a lifetime of wind and glare. And they are quite large now so they are going to remove those. And I'm hopeful that they will clear up my vision a little bit.'

Living in a small country town in a remote area has made it easier to deal with the practicalities of her vision loss, she says. Karumba is a community. And everyone looks out for each other.

'Here, I go to the pool every day and a girl that I swim with picks me up. My sister lives down the road. If she's going shopping I go with her. Everyone's sort of aware of your situation, so, you know, it's easier being here.

'No one gets to be my age without a cross to bear. I'm really fit for my age. Most people I know my age are getting plastic hips and knee replacements or they are having cancer treatment so I'm not going to whine.'

Every month for the past four years, Lyne has travelled to Cairns for eye treatment. Sometimes she flies, but often she takes the 11-hour bus ride.

'There's four stops along the way. And over the years you get to know everyone in the roadhouses so it's really quite social,' she says.

Lyne is a natural storyteller and loves a chat. But she wasn't always that way. She was incredibly shy as a child, and had a stutter. And she says she always felt stupid, after leaving school at the age of 12.

It all started in 1965 when her brother, Steve, was born. He was youngest of Lyne's siblings. The last to be born. She'd had two other sisters already. But it was a difficult birth. The nurses told her father, John, that her mother, Ida, wouldn't survive it.

'I'll never forget the look on his face,' she says. 'There's no way he could have kept us together. He was looking at my sisters and me, and a brand-new baby.'

In the end, Ida survived. But something had shifted in John, a veteran of the Korean War. A few months later he came home with a Toyota and a caravan and told the girls they'd never have to go back to school again. They were going to travel around Australia.

'Mum wrote us all out notes that we took to school the next day,' Lyne remembers. 'They said: Lyne won't be coming back to school. Lyne is finishing school. This is her last day. That was it. I remember my teacher, Mrs Cousins, said: "Oh. What are you going to be doing?" I said, "We are going to be travelling around." She replied, "What are you going to do for school?" And I said, "Correspondence."'

She pauses.

'She must have had an inkling. She just said, "Look, if you go to school you can make something of your life. If you don't, you will just end up working in a factory."

'And I went, "Oh ... okay." She said, "Write to me." So I did write to her for a long time.'

The family travelled around Australia for the next seven years. Lyne's father wanted to turn his back on civilisation entirely. He didn't trust schools. Or doctors. They travelled on remote, unsealed roads. They lived in the bush and kept to themselves. When people started asking too many questions, they'd moved to another town.

'He had this hatred of being cold so he just said we are going to follow the sun now,' she says. 'And that's what we did. We'd just pull up at a river and Mum would put a fish trap in, and we'd stay there for another month. We just travelled and when we ran out of money, Dad would pull up and go into a pub and then just say, "Right, we've got a farm," and we'd go to a farm and we'd all pick grapes for a few months and then we'd move on.'

They wouldn't even stay in caravan parks. Lyne's father would always park 20 kilometres out of town.

When they'd first arrive in a new town they all had jobs to do. Ida and Lyne's older sister Sandy would get the groceries. Her father, John, would buy alcohol. And bullets for the gun to hunt their food. It was Lyne's job to trade their second-hand books for new ones at a 'swap shop'.

'I would go in, I would go through every single book in the swap shop,' she says. 'Dad always liked those Larry and Stretch cowboy books. Mum liked horror stories. I'd get comics for the kids and then I'd go through all the books in the shop. I educated myself on books.

'I didn't make friends easily and I was a really backwards sort of kid at school, so I was really glad when we left,' she says. 'I'm 64 now. I don't think I really came out of my shell until I went to university when I was 50 and I stopped feeling like I was uneducated. That was when I learned to talk to people, because I spent most of my life thinking I was stupid. Or uneducated. Less than equal.'

She hated being different.

'I'll never forget we went into Mildura – we were picking wine grapes. I was 12,' she says. 'You'd go down just when the sun came up and you finished when the sun came down, picking all day. You get a lot of secateur scratches on your hands and then the purple dye seeps into them and then your hands just look wrecked. I'll never forget, it was horrible.

Going to Mildura to stock up on groceries and the woman was looking at me like I was a normal person, at the checkout.

'She really seemed quite friendly, and then I had to put my hand out to get change and she looked down and saw my hand and the look of horror and pity, because I was so young. You don't want that horror or pity and you don't want to be different. Everyone spends their life wanting to be unique and an individual, but when you grow up really different you want to just blend in and be like everybody else.'

Looking back now, though, she sees her childhood as a positive experience.

'I like it at sea because you just get very close to a few people. After a few weeks you don't even have to talk. Everyone finds their own little place on the boat to go and just be quiet for a while. It's like you've got a nice family. It reminds me of being back in the caravan, when we were travelling.

'It was a privileged life. I used to walk in the bush. No one ever kept tabs. I'd leave in the morning ... I wouldn't get back for hours. It was absolute freedom. In the end you learn to love it and then you learn to need it. To really need that.'

When the family reached Mount Isa, seven years into their travels, Lyne's father asked them to make a decision – to stay or to head north. It was the first time they'd been consulted on the trip. He'd heard of Karumba, 600 kilometres up the road. He'd dreamed of catching a big fish. Or he could work in a mine in Mount Isa.

'We all knew he wanted to go up there but my sisters and I wanted to stay in Mount Isa because it was civilisation and I was 18 then,' she says. 'But we just said what Dad wanted to hear: let's go up there. It was all dirt. Took ages. It was just a trip from hell.'

Finally they arrived in Karumba. They had spent their last $20 on petrol to get there. It was 1972 and there was barely a soul around.

'He just said, "Oh, it's a bit busy", so he drove across the salt flats, and we ended up living out at the point for a while and eventually we moved up into the mangroves.

'When you're 18 and you're up there with your mum and dad, and the sandflies and the mosquitoes and the heat, and the town's over that way; you're looking at the lights at night and that's where you'd really rather be.'

It was a rough camp. There was no water. It took her father 14 years to lay down a concrete slab. They had a solar panel, which gave them some power, and a kerosene fridge.

'It took a long time to appreciate it. It's funny, I love it here. When we first came here I remember arriving and looking out and thinking, my God, where have we come? It was like hell. But it's very subtle and it took a fair few years but I get it now; I get it.'

Lyne says at that time Karumba was like the Wild West.

'It was like the end of the world. It was like the end of the known world,' she says. 'It was just a frontier, lawless town. It frightened me. I just couldn't relate to it. It was all dirt, dust. People living in rainwater tanks, cars, caravans. There was about two or three houses for the factory managers.

'My sisters and I started to warm to the town. We drove up to the water's edge and looked across at the prawn factory just at smoko time. And suddenly there was an endless stream of young people in white aprons and gumboots. All looked deliriously happy, all spilled out to go to the shop. It didn't look like it was going to be such a bad place then, or as isolated as some of the places we'd been used to.'

Many of the people working on the trawlers were dodging the draft for the Vietnam War. There were women fleeing domestic violence. Karumba was the sort of place you could go to hide away from the world.

'You could come here and never be seen again,' she says. 'That was in the days when a driver's licence was a piece of paper, typed on a typewriter. There was no photographic ID. You could open three bank accounts in Karumba under different names if you wanted to.'

There was a post office. A police station. A clinic. The factory.

'It was booming. Everyone was making a lot of money. If we'd learned something as a family it was how to work hard for short periods,' she says. 'In those days $80 a week was the weekly standard wage and if you were very fast in the prawn factory you could make $360 per week. It was huge.'

The sisters got jobs in the factory. Their father bought a little dingy and would fish out the front.

It was in the prawn factory she met Mick. And fell in love with a life on the trawlers. And, ironically, travel. She would work the prawn seasons and save up money to see the world.

'Once I started working on boats you'd go out to sea, make some money and go overseas,' she says. 'And each time I came back I appreciated the isolation more. Because here it doesn't matter if you are young, you are old, you are disabled, you're a dog lover. It doesn't matter who you are or what you are; you are somebody in this town. You are just one of the faceless grey masses when you are in a city. It's a funny place. Scratch the surface and we are all a close-knit bunch.'

When she had her two daughters, Simone and Myra, she put them through school as a single mother, and paid for it by working on boats. Then she went to university. She's done two degrees. She writes short stories now, and has won prizes for them.

'If I hadn't led the life I've led, I don't think I'd have stories to tell my grandchildren,' she says.

'Because of my eyesight I can't go and do long seasons,' she says. Instead, she goes and talks to the new recruits, the young women – mostly backpackers – who are making their own first voyage on the fleet of boats.

'There's always new crew these days,' she says. 'Every year they'll end up with about five or six brand-new girls that have never been to sea. So I'll go down and help them put their stores away and stop freaking out and tell them – because no one tells them – what to do.

'Everyone's busy because they all arrive a few days before they leave on a two-month or a four-month trip, and they are just busy. Guys are putting the nets on board and the skipper is getting the computers all run up and there's always drama. And the girls, they just freak out. A lot of them don't make it, they leave before the boat even goes. The girls that are experienced now, they're all between 50 and 60 years old. They will come back each year but we are all going to die out soon.'

Lyne reckons she'll stick in Karumba for now.

'I really like the harsh landscape here. And I like people that choose to live in isolated places. You can have your petty squabbles, and we do. But when the chips are down, all that disappears. Everyone pulls together. They are good people.

'I like that I've lived in a lot of other places. My dad used to say, "Lyne, get out there. Travel. Look at other places, because only if you've put a foot in a lot of different worlds can you make an informed decision on where you want to stand."

'Had I never left here I'd probably feel a bit more like a bogan than I do. But because I've travelled, I've been around. I choose to live here.'

16
Thursday Island

Location: Thursday Island is an island in the Torres Strait, about 39 km north of Cape York.

Population: 2938

Aired: The *Back Roads* episode on Thursday Island aired on Monday 19 December 2016. It was the fourth episode in the second series.

SWEAT IS POURING DOWN Elsie Seriat's face as she makes her fifth climb up Milman Hill, on Thursday Island, in the Torres Strait. It's a humid, hot morning. She can hear the sounds of children playing, crickets, and the mocking laughter of kookaburras as she zigzags up the incline. Slowly. Shuffling ever more slowly.

She's 29, but her body feels older today. Strands of her black curly hair are sticking to her round face. Usually her infectious wide grin matches the smile of her eyes, but today they are both pained. Her straight white teeth are locked in grimace. Her legs hurt. Her entire body feels done. Every step is an effort.

Enough. But there are eight more ascents ahead. One kilometre each. That's eight more kilometres, uphill. Impossible. And crazy.

'I'm quitting,' she tells her running partner.

He raises an eyebrow at her but doesn't speak.

'I don't want to do it,' she cries. 'I hate it! I hate you.'

He lets her unload.

It's been a massive few weeks for Elsie. It's all been building to this moment. A reckoning. She's just been chosen to train for and run in the New York Marathon in six months time.

Excitement. Trepidation. She's one of 12 Indigenous men and women selected for their potential as leaders from around Australia. It's all part of champion marathon runner Robert de Castella's Indigenous Marathon Project.

Thoughts swirl foggily in Elsie's head as reality sets in. One step, and then another. What on earth was she thinking? She's only on her second training run and already broken.

Elsie is also missing her sister dearly. Her pregnant younger sister, Maletta, has been evacuated to Townsville, 1500 kilometres to the south, where she's delivered a premature baby girl, Elma Faith, at just 23 weeks. Elsie feels alone: her mother, May, has gone to be with Maletta. And here she is training for a marathon. Until the doubt got too great, and broke into an outpouring of emotion halfway up Milman Hill.

'He didn't say anything,' Elsie recalls of her training partner, Brenton Koch. 'Nothing. He just let me talk and then he said to me, "Are you done?" and I said "Yep", and he said, "Keep on running". And then I just kept on running. Because I'd already let it all out.'

It was March 2014. She didn't know it, but those minutes would prove to be pivotal in Elsie's life. And for the life and health of her beloved Torres Strait Island community.

Elsie's commitment to running, and her determination to continue training on that day, set off a series of changes in her community. Which rippled into other changes. More and more people got active, and involved. Elsie calls it a running revolution.

'I wanted to be a change agent,' she says. 'I wanted people to see me and want to be part of this change. When I look back now, when I think about what's happening on Thursday Island, it's all what we wanted it to be and what we wanted it to look like. People are slowly getting into the idea.'

Running is still new for the island but it's more about getting them out and getting them active. That's what really matters.

'Young and old, everyone's out exercising.'

Thursday Island is one of 16 inhabited islands in the Torres Strait, an island chain off the northern tip of Queensland. Elsie was born and bred here. She's from Sipingur on Mabuiag Island in the Torres Strait. She's part of the Kaygas clan of the Moegi Buway tribe. English is her third language, though she's fluent.

Her connection to her family and her community is deep, as is her joy at the impact her journey has already had on the island. These days it's a common sight to see women and men in shorts and donning a 'DEADLY RUNNERS' singlet with the Torres Strait Islander and Aboriginal flags on them running or exercising around the island.

It wasn't always that way. It only started to shift just a month or two before Elsie found herself repeatedly climbing Milman Hill. Elsie had been working in administration in the medical records section of Queensland's health department. She'd been there for 14 years. As a result, she was pretty aware of the health statistics in her community. It was something that weighed on her mind. High numbers of Torres Strait Islanders had diabetes. Heart problems. Kidney disease.

Elsie was also keen to lose weight herself.

'I've always been an active person in my community. I've played a lot of contact sports,' she says. 'But I was a big, really big girl and I wanted to lose weight.'

When she was younger, she'd played basketball. Then it was rugby league. In 2009 she was selected to play rugby league for Queensland in the women's team. She represented the state for the next four years. But training was only once a week. She felt she wasn't losing any weight. So she joined a boot camp training session, with a personal trainer. It helped a little. But she was upset only a handful of the participants were Indigenous.

'I'm like, where are all my people? It would be nice to see them here,' she says. 'Life expectancy is a major issue. You see all these young people dying. Dying from preventable disease. I wanted more locals to be involved in the boot camp but they wouldn't come because they were either ashamed or they didn't have the money to pay.'

So she started her own free exercise program in the community, with one of her aunties. They called it Free to Fitness and their motto was 'Willpower, know no obstacle'.

'It was just great to have all the locals involved, like all my aunties and my cousins and people who haven't exercised for a long time. It all started with that. Realising we are a small community and we can all help each other. We were so exposed to football and basketball and volleyball, but there were other sports that we could have done.'

She heard about the Indigenous Marathon Project (IMP), and thought she'd give it a go.

The IMP is a not-for-profit health organisation, set up by former world champion marathon runner Robert 'Deeks' de Castella in 2009 to help develop inspirational Indigenous leaders through running. More than 75 of its participants have finished an international marathon while taking part.

'I wouldn't have even thought of running a marathon,' Elsie admits. 'I've come from a zero running background. Running wasn't my thing.'

She even used to hide during cross-country events when she was at school.

But in early 2014, the IMP proposed a visit to the Torres Strait and called for expressions of interest from people interested in running the New York Marathon later that year. Elsie was drawn to a line on the IMP website which said the organisation aimed to create inspirational Indigenous leaders.

'I read what the other graduates who had finished the

project, what they had done in their communities when they came back home. When I read it I thought I could be that person. I want to be that change in my community. That's why I did it. I'll give this a go.'

Elsie tried to start training. She'd run for a bit, but would walk as soon as she heard a car coming. She was embarrassed. But the tryouts were looming. She needed to be able to run three kilometres, and she hadn't run that far before. Fortunately, she kept bumping into an acquaintance who wanted to help. Brenton Koch was a local triathlete.

'One time I was walking around the island and he saw me and stopped and said, "I hear you're training for a marathon. I want to help you. I can help you train." I said that's fine, I know what I'm doing,' she says.

'Then after that I kept bumping into him. He'd be like, "I'm still waiting for you, Elsie. Whenever you are ready". I'm like, that's fine, mate. He was just in my face all the time. And so then I said yes.'

Brenton was a tough, disciplined trainer. It was just what she needed.

'He was super hard. He was, like, so cruel to me. But I think it was for the best.'

The first hurdle would be the tryouts for acceptance into the marathon project. They started cycling four times a week together. Four laps of the island – 20 kilometres in total. 'It was a godsend for me,' Elsie says.

Then one day just before the tryouts he told her they were going to run up Milman Hill. Thirteen times. Zigzagging the steep one kilometre to the top.

'It took me eight hours on a Saturday. One whole working day,' she emphasises. 'He did it with me. He was in pain as well.'

On the way up she thought a lot about her eating habits.

'I thought about my eating then, of trying to get it right,' she says. 'I was drinking a lot of alcohol. Soft drink. I was cursing it all.'

Even so, on tryout day, Elsie didn't really think much of it. She just thought she'd give it a go.

'I was the biggest girl at the tryouts,' she recalls. 'I invited everyone I knew to come down but only six people came down to the tryouts and when they rocked up they were like, fit as. And I was like, no. I'm not going to make it.'

The women had to run three kilometres in 500-metre straights. Up and back. Up and back.

'I could see them running in front of me,' Elsie says. 'Then I could see them walking. And I was like, no, I'm not going to walk, even though I'm shuffling, I'm not walking. So I just shuffled the whole way. I was in so much pain. Three kilometres – my first ever long run.'

After that, they each had a one-on-one interview with Robert de Castella.

'I said that I wanted to give back to my community and I wanted to be a role model, for my generation and for my nieces and nephew. For the generation that's coming up.

'All that gets back to life expectancy. I want people to live longer. Especially my cousins, my friends, my family. I want them to see their children, and their grandchildren. And if they're lucky, their great-grandchildren. My grandfather's 88 years old and he's gotten to see his great-grandkids. But that generation of my mum's – my uncles and aunties – they're all dying. They're not even getting to 70. Hopefully we can change that by promoting what we eat now, and what my grandfather has done to live that longer life, by exercising, being active, working in the garden. He's never been a smoker or drinker.'

Her words – and her clear gritty determination not to give in on the run – sealed the deal. Someone from the IMP rang to follow up a week or so later. She had been successful, as had Harold Matthew, the only male who'd tried out.

'When the announcement was official, people were, like beeping their horns and saying "Woah! New York! Woohoo," when they saw me.'

By then Elsie had been training regularly for several months. But her next big test would be a ten-kilometre run in Canberra in three weeks time.

So her training partner, Brenton, made her run up Milman Hill again. Thirteen times. This time with huge containers of water, representing all the weight she'd lost in the previous couple of months: twelve kilograms.

It was here she became unstuck. Momentarily. Her mother and sister were in Townsville. And the training was tough.

'It was more about making a difference than it was about running,' she says, of her motivation. 'When I started to train, I was like, no. I don't want to do this any more. It's so hard.'

Eventually, she made it through the intense session and went home. Maletta had needed an emergency caesarean. She had a little girl, Elma Faith.

'But the baby was born with a chronic lung disease,' Elsie says.

The prognosis wasn't good. Doctors were trying to prepare her younger sister for the painful reality that her daughter probably wouldn't make it. To Elsie, they felt so far away. She longed to be there for her sister.

It was with that background that Elsie's intense training continued. She threw herself into it. Even so, the event in Canberra snuck up fast.

She told Brenton she was filled with doubt. 'I said to him, I don't know if I can do this,' she says. 'He was like, you are going to be fine. You are fit enough now.'

There were 11 others, including Harold, in the IMP program meeting in Canberra. Elsie ran the entire ten kilometres without stopping. Six weeks later, she ran her first half marathon. Twenty-one kilometres on the Gold Coast. In all, there would be four running camps in the seven months leading up to New York Marathon Day.

Back on the island, Elsie kept up her training with Brenton and Harold. 'Some days we all trained together because I was still struggling when I went back home running,' she says. 'It was so intense I didn't know what I was doing. I was crying at some stages, asking why am I doing this? I can't run. I can't do this. I had thousands of excuses with my shoes, my legs, and eventually I ran out of excuses and just did it.'

By then the running revolution had taken off on the island. Each Sunday there was a community fun walk around the island. When Elsie and Harold ran the Gold Coast half marathon, there was a group back on Thursday Island doing a run too.

Elsie mainly trained in the morning. At 6am. It was still dark, but that didn't matter: she couldn't really see, anyway.

'I'd leave my glasses at home because I hate running with stuff,' she says. 'I don't wear a hat. Nothing. I just run. Not even keys. You don't have to lock your doors here. When I'm running, I'm blind. Like literally. I can see figures and stuff when you come close.'

Her sister and mother were still in Townsville caring for Elma, who remained in hospital. Elsie hadn't yet met her newborn niece.

So when her next big run – a 30-kilometre run in Alice Springs – came up in August, she decided to surprise them en route. So she flew to Cairns, and then drove 350 kilometres south to Townsville.

'Coming from a tiny island, it was the craziest thing I've ever done – drive,' she says.

'All these semi-trailers and road trains! I wouldn't have been able to do it if it wasn't part of what I'd already been exposed to, within the project. I was just totally out of my comfort zone. That's what the project does, it takes you out of your comfort zone to do things that you've never done before.'

When she met Elma, the tiny baby was hooked up to a series of machines in the hospital that were helping her to breathe.

'It was the best decision that I could have ever made, to see her,' Elsie says. 'She was all plugged up to these breathing machines, and here I was thinking Alice Springs was going to be so tough. Thirty kilometres – I've never done it. The longest I'd run was 25 kilometres in training. But seeing Elma, I thought wow, Elma's depending on this machine. She's having it tougher than me. So I saw Elma and got to tell her what I was doing and stuff. Have a yarn with her.'

Then she drove back to Cairns and flew to Alice Springs.

'I ran with her name on my arm and I dedicated that run to her,' she says. 'When it was really tough and I wanted to stop and quit, I'd look down and kiss my hand and say, come on Elma, push through. Get her through the race. And I did it. I did 32 kilometres instead of 30 – I got lost and missed my turn. But it was all worth it. The best thing was to ring back to Townsville and tell them I did it for her. I didn't even stop, though I wanted to. I needed to finish.'

She flew back home with a final eight-week push to the 42-kilometre New York Marathon.

New York was incredible, surreal, says Elsie: 'Just like the movies with the yellow cabs everywhere, beeping their horns. "Get out of my way!" It's just so busy.'

Her mother bought a plane ticket and told her she would watch her from the 35-kilometre mark. 'I couldn't stop. I just waved and said I'll see you at the finish because I was in pain. My mind was telling me to stop and quit,' she says. 'Sometimes shame is a big thing in our culture. We get told that we can't do it. And so being there, running in New York, every single kilometre I knew I wasn't alone. Even though back home it was the early hours of the morning, some of my friends and family were up watching every step of me running.'

So she kept running. And running.

'Just for my family and for my community. And to tell everyone that anything is possible if you put in your heart and your mind. You can do it.'

She usually hated running with any personal items. But for the marathon, she carried the Torres Strait Islander flag in a bumbag around her waist. She took it out and ran with it for the final two kilometres. She finished with jelly legs, and a respectable time of four hours, 36 minutes.

'I got to the finish line and I saw Rob de Castella. I didn't think that I would cry but I just broke down.'

When she flew home, it felt like the entire island was waiting at the wharf on Thursday Island to greet her.

'To see all your family and friends down there with posters – I thought I'd finished all my cries in New York but I was still crying. It was just so good to see everyone.'

But not everyone was there. Elsie's sister and newborn niece were still in Townsville, so their mother May flew back down to be with them. It had been six months since Elma's birth.

'Mum rang three weeks later to say, your sister needs you, bubba is not doing well,' Elsie says. 'I said I'm on the next flight. I literally dropped everything and flew down to Cairns.

'During the transit from Cairns to Townsville we lost Elma. She couldn't hold on. I guess it was just too hard.

'Maletta had Elma waiting for me before they put her in the mortuary. When I walked in it was so hard. I just had to thank her and be strong, and say thank you. Because if anything had have happened to you in my six months of training I don't think I would have finished the marathon. I showed Elma my medal. And took photos with her. And I was able to thank my sister for being so strong. It just happened so fast.

'Coming from a Christian upbringing, I believe God put Elma here for a reason. I'm going to continue to do what I'm doing. I'm not going to stop, even though there are times when I want to quit. It's for her that I'm doing what I'm doing.'

Maletta followed in Elsie's footsteps and ran the New York Marathon in 2017.

Thursday Island now has its own running festival, held every October.

'When we got home, we kept on running.'

Elsie started a running group, the Deadly Beginners. She'd lost 20 kilograms during her training, and inspired others to join her. She ran several successful groups, training more than 60 people to run five kilometres – one lap of the island – over eight weeks. Her mother, May, was among those who signed up. As more and more people signed up and became active, others became interested.

'Running was a therapy. And it was eventually becoming a therapy for me. You just go out there and do it by yourself and you can think about a lot of things for yourself.'

She also met her partner, Neville Johnston. He'd started running too. He ran a marathon ten months after they met.

Since Elsie and Harold's successful marathon in 2014, the IMP has picked a representative from Thursday Island every year. But Elsie and Neville have moved away to Canberra. For now.

Elsie got a job working with the IMP, supporting all the previous graduates around the country to help them realise their dreams post-marathon in a program called Front Runners. She gets to visit Thursday Island semi-regularly, so she hasn't been too homesick. Yet.

'I always said that I was going to move away from home but I didn't think it would happen so soon,' she says.

'The hardest thing before moving away was the marathon. But moving away now was the hardest thing, to leave my family behind and take on this new journey.'

The marathon helped her take the first steps.

'Moving away this short time that I've been here, I feel like I've got so much to give back now. I'm so excited that I've been exposed to all these things which I can see being implemented in our community and can work.'

Looking back, if she could speak to herself struggling up Milman Hill and wanting to quit, she'd tell herself to keep going.

'I would say to myself, believe in yourself. You can't quit. Don't look back. Just keep moving forward.'

17

A hairdressing journey

Location: Hairdresser Lyn Westbury lives in Innisfail,
Queensland. But every six weeks or so she travels along
the remote Savannah Way in Far North Queensland to
Normanton with her mobile hairdressing salon.
Aired: *Back Roads* joined Lyn and her assistant, Fil Stewart,
on their hairdressing trip in June 2016. The episode aired in
the second series of *Back Roads*, on 3 December 2016.

LYN WESTBURY WATCHES AS a caravan approaches and whizzes
past her vehicle.

'What's this? A Crusader?' she asks. 'Here comes another
one. Forty-nine. We've seen lots today.'

There's a shout from behind the vehicle: 'Forty-eight!'

'No, that's forty-nine,' Lyn counters, peering over her
black-rimmed glassed at the open back door.

'Forty-eight!' comes the reply.

Lyn takes a sip of water from a plastic water bottle. And waits. As you'd expect, her short hair is shiny and immaculate. She's been a hairdresser for decades. It's a warm brown, which turns burgundy when it catches the light.

Another caravan passes.

'Fifty,' says the voice out the back.

'Woo hoo!' Lyn smiles.

Another vehicle passes.

'Fifty-one!' they both shout in unison.

Lyn's parked off to the side of the highway, waiting for her friend Fil Stewart to hop back inside.

Fil is 78. Long retired. With gentle, soft skin, white hair and a generous smile. Grandmotherly.

They're on about day four of a 1600-kilometre, nine-day trip across the top of Queensland. They've spent hours and hours together. And they get along. It's Thelma and Louise, with caravan spotting.

They count the numerous caravans they pass. Or they sing. Mainly ballads, like John Denver's 'Take Me Home, Country Road'. It helps them stay alert to hazards such as wildlife and cattle on the roads.

It's 2015 and *Back Roads* has joined them on the trip. They make the journey every six weeks or so, along Queensland's outback Savannah Way, stopping at towns and properties en route, as a one-stop-shop mobile hairdressing team.

The car is packed to the hilt. Shopping bags, clothes baskets. Crammed. Everything they'll need for the next week on the road. Mirrors. Scissors. Teabags. Fil's been making the trip for about five years or so. Lyn's been doing it for 15.

'We count caravans, yes we do. Yes, along the way. And then when we see the big road trains, we count all the road trains with all the cattle,' Lyn says. 'I just love it. I just feel as though we're all getting older and there's more to life than just sitting in a little town, and I just want to be out there and just live my life.'

Remote stretches are familiar to Lyn. She grew up in the 1960s on an isolated sugar cane property in East Feluga, about 50 kilometres south of Innisfail.

'My mum and dad had to clear the land from nothing. It was pretty tough then,' she says. They lived in a shed, using a generator for heating, with a kerosene fridge and gas stove. They had a tiny six-inch TV, which came on at night. Each day Lyn and her siblings would get a lift with their mother along a dirt road for the ten kilometres to their uncle's place, and then ride another four kilometres to school on their bikes.

'When it flooded, she used to take us to our uncle's place by tractor,' Lyn recalls. 'I grew up with a sense of adventure. I think that's why I can relate to a lot of the families on the properties.'

She didn't get to a hair salon until much later, but as a girl she was fascinated with hairdressing. She'd chomp into her doll's hair with an old pair of scissors.

'I only had really, really long hair,' Lyn says. 'We never went to town. Tully was about 20 kilometres away. Mum used to phone the grocery order through to the local supermarket and Dad went to town on a Friday to pay bills, go to the bank and pick up the groceries while we were at school. In those days hair salons were very few and far between. Mum used to cut the ends off my hair and cut my fringe. I look at school photos now and think, oh my gawd.'

Their one big outing each year was to the local show.

'Mum used to make us a new outfit every year to go to the show,' Lyn remembers. 'She made all our clothes and taught us to sew.'

When she left high school, Lyn gained a hairdressing apprenticeship in Innisfail, where her aunt lived. Soon after, she met her husband-to-be, Barry.

'Having many leaking taps in the salon, we used to call on the plumbers down the road and Barry would always come. Now I know why. I used to park my car in the car park near his workshop and I walked past there every day,' she says. 'I think he may have had his eye on me. We've been married 40 years this year.'

They have two children, Glen and Karyn.

It was the chance purchase of a car that led Lyn to leave her salon business temporarily and embark on a road trip. It was 2003, and her teenage son, Glen, had saved up to buy a second-hand LandCruiser. It was in Karumba, in Far North Queensland, 720 kilometres west of Innisfail.

'The young guy that was selling it, he said, "If you meet us halfway in Georgetown I'll bring it down so you can have a look at it,"' Lyn says.

After the sale was agreed, the vendor drove it to Innisfail for a roadworthy inspection. He decided to wait in the hairdressing salon, and got chatting to Lyn.

'He said, "Lyn, we own the supermarket in Karumba and there's a hairdressing part in it. No one is using it. Why don't you come over and give it a go?"'

It was not just the banks closing their doors in struggling outback towns – hairdressing salons were shutting down too. Her daughter Karyn was working alongside her in the salon in Innisfail, and they both went on the first few trips together.

'When you're a country person yourself, you can relate to all these people, and how isolated you really were too as a child,' Lyn says. 'We went to Karumba and it branched out from there. When people knew what I was doing, they asked me, "Why don't you stop here, why don't you stop there?" and that's how it all started. The trips got longer and longer.'

Places like Mount Surprise, Georgetown, Croydon and Normanton were added to the itinerary. Stops were timed to coincide with debutante balls, weddings and rodeos. Her favourite thing is the regular catch-ups with the people she meets. Over the years, they've become friends.

'I had a salon for 20 years and I decided I loved training all my girls and that, but I just loved coming to the outback,' Lyn says. 'Everyone is so different and every town is so different. Everyone has got their little stories to tell you. Sometimes I think I should have been a psychologist because that goes with hairdressing. Everyone, they just confide in you with their little stories and what's happening in their life. And if you just reassure them about a few little things, they're happy.

'A lot of them that come in off the property, all they've got is men and they just love to come in and have a chat and have a cup of tea and just have a little bit of female company.'

Some women drive an hour or more to see her.

Fil says, 'You just sit there, listen, have a yarn, make them a cup of tea. They come in off stations and haven't seen each other for a while. Have a chat. And keep making lots of cups of tea. That's the beauty of it all.'

Today they're at the CWA Hall in Normanton, in the Gulf of Carpentaria. It's the last stop on their trip with *Back Roads*, and the town's big rodeo event begins tonight.

Lyn is painting dye onto client Shannon Gallagher's hair with a brush. Her head is already peppered with folded bits of aluminium foil. Lyn has a look of intense concentration. Fil is standing beside her.

'I'm glad I'm doing this, actually,' Shannon tells them. 'It's an hour to relax.' Shannon has been busy organising the town's rodeo.

'I don't know what we'd do without you,' she tells Lyn. Then, to *Back Roads* host Heather Ewart, she adds, 'She's been doing this for a few years now and she knows what she's doing. It seems like such a small thing but it's huge. When you don't have a hairdresser it's massive to have to go out of town to get this sort of stuff done. You'd be amazed. Sometimes being involved with recruitment and that sort of thing in various organisations, how often women who are interviewing for jobs want to know if there's a hairdresser in town. That's something that influences people's decisions to come and want to live here sometimes, you know.

'It's a super, super service. I don't know what we'd do without you, Lyn. I'm rapping you up a bit here but it really is a great service for our town.'

Lyn replies, 'And I loves you all, Shannon.'

'Oh, good on ya,' Shannon laughs.

Fil was a hairdressing client of Lyn's for 20 years. Now she spends her time answering the phone, washing the towels and importantly, making cups of tea for everyone.

'She's been a client of mine since 1990 and when she finished the job that she had, and she was on her own, I just said to her would you like to come? And she goes, yes,' Lyn says. She's met some of her friends that she went to school with and they've caught up after all these years. She teaches them crocheting, and they share patterns and everything like that. She is like a mother to me; she has got four children of her own but sometimes we have some very big deep and meaningful discussions along our way.'

Fil likes to keep things pretty neat. In fact, that's how she came to know Lyn. She'd drop into Lyn's salon on her way home in Innisfail and have a cup of tea and a chat. Then she started straightening things up to help out.

'I like method, if you know what I mean,' Fil says. 'Everything's got to be where it should be so that, with Lyn's business, you know she's got to keep the ball rolling like that. And I've got to make sure that all her bowls and brushes are all clean. I just scrub and rub and have everything there for her so that she can keep going.'

The days can be quite intense, with dozens of women, men and children waiting for their time in the chair.

'I must say I'm one of those, come one o'clock, two o'clock, just a quick power nap, and think, okay, I'm fine now, I'll keep going,' Fil says. 'Like I always say to Lyn, it only lasts for seven, eight days. I can go home then and I can sleep till I want to.'

She counts Lyn as a good friend.

'Hairdressing's been her life for so long and it's just something she loves. I think that's part of human nature, isn't it, to feel wanted, to feel needed. I think Lyn would be on the same page as me. You just love giving. I always say to people, you know, there's plenty of love here, come on, come and get it.'

The road trips were a huge step out of Fil's comfort zone. She was born in Innisfail, and is still there at 78. Her husband of 43 years, Bobbie, died in 2003. She has four children, five grandchildren, and three great-grandchildren across Australia.

She says Innisfail was all she knew until she started travelling about five or six years ago. The trips with Lyn were a big part of changing that. By 2018, Fil had retired from the long road trips. 'It was time to pack up and retire,' Fil says. 'I was getting too old and it was catching up. I thoroughly enjoyed doing it. It was a real experience,' she says. 'From a little country town, you'd never think of doing it.'

But the adventure still continues for Lyn. Her husband, Barry, now joins her on the road.

'I still have got a lot of living to do.'

18

Winton (and Middleton)

Location: Winton is 1355 km north-west of Brisbane.
Middleton is 169 km west of Winton.

Population: 875

Aired: Winton was one of the first towns *Back Roads* visited
when the series began in 2015. During the episode, the crew
also filmed in the tiny settlement of Middleton.

DAVID ELLIOTT'S BROW IS furrowed in fervent concentration.

'I really do need the picture that came on the box,' Judy,
his wife, quips.

The couple are piecing together a jigsaw – from a pile of
rock. They're fragments of 95-million-year-old dinosaur bone.
It's proving somewhat tricky. But it's an art that graziers
David and Judy Elliott are well-versed in, as they kneel in the
hard, dusty earth on a sheep and cattle property near Winton

in the middle of the vast Queensland outback, about 1400 kilometres from Brisbane.

It's 2015 and *Back Roads* has come to film the operation. Over the past 16 years – with an assortment of dedicated volunteers and staff – David and Judy have gradually uncovered the world's largest collection of Australian dinosaur fossils in their backyard and on neighbouring properties.

David has a narrow, tanned face shaded by a beaten brown cowboy hat. He's wearing a light-coloured work shirt with a large dinosaur logo above the left pocket. 'Australian Age of Dinosaurs', it reads proudly. Judy is wearing a black and pink singlet and jeans, and has short brown and grey speckled hair.

In all, they have found bones belonging to more than 30 different individuals, mostly vegetarian long-necked sauropods, with an eclectic smattering of names from Olga and Oliver to Bob and Clancy, depending on the whim of the owner of the property where the bones were found.

There is even a dinosaur named Packer: his bones were uncovered the same day the late media tycoon Kerry Packer died.

'It just sneaks up on you,' David says, of their obsession, noting that if he'd known how much time and work this prehistoric passion would consume, he would have dismissed it long ago as all too hard. But it's like eating an elephant, he adds, mystifyingly.

'You know: how do you eat an elephant?' he asks. 'It's easy – just one bite at a time and just keep eating it – and sooner or later you're going to eat him aren't you? Yeah, I'll probably finish the tail; I'm halfway down the first leg. By taking things in stages you can get it into bite-size chunks that you can handle.'

The couple are chewing slowly. They've developed a natural history museum to house the collection, called the Australian Age of Dinosaurs. A countless stream of volunteers make the pilgrimage to the remote site each year, to prepare, preserve and dig for bones. In addition to the impressive dinosaur bone collection, they have uncovered ancient teeth, turtles, small crocodile bones and evidence of flying reptiles.

Back onsite, a gust of hot wind sends the sides of the yellow shade marquee behind the couple flapping impatiently.

'There is just so much missing here, and there are no chunks that are anything like it at all,' he mumbles, picking up a piece. 'Have you got the other end of this bit?'

The Australian Age of Dinosaurs museum holds a dinosaur dig over three weeks each year, with up to 13 diggers at a time. They receive expert advice and guidance from the Queensland Museum.

It all started in 1999, when David spotted something unusual during a sheep muster.

'I always wanted to find a dinosaur bone,' he says. 'I knew straight away what it was. I just knew it was dinosaur bone so I jammed the brakes on and turned around as fast as I could. It was a pile of rocks and it was definitely bone. I took some coordinates on a couple of prickly bushes so I knew I could get my way back there, which is all I really needed to do and I went back to the sheep.'

It took another 18 months and a flood before he recovered the pieces of thigh bone.

'It was so exciting,' he remembers. 'It's funny; we find so many dinosaur bones now and it's just becoming a little bit – oh yeah, there's another one, you know, but back then you found a piece of dinosaur bone and you loved it. It made your day; made your week.'

The dinosaur was named Elliott after the fourth-generation sheep farmer – but a typing error left it with just one 'T' – not two – when the discovery was first publicised. The story spread like wildfire, and the misspelled name stuck.

'Elliot' was for a time Australia's largest dinosaur, before being eclipsed by a fellow Queenslander, a monster called Cooper. By 2005, the Australian Age of Dinosaurs team was finding so many bones they decided to set up their own lab.

'I didn't want to see all of these fossils leave the district and not be able to do something for the district – I find that unacceptable,' David says. 'There were a lot of hard decisions for me because I was still running a property. I just realised that what we were doing is not about Winton. It's not even about western Queensland. We had a national treasure in our backyard.'

He has now accepted that dinosaurs are firmly in his life to stay.

'It drives me now,' he shrugs. 'I miss the property work but, you know, it's only a couple of months ago I went out and gave the boys a hand to crutch a mob of sheep one day. After a couple of runs my back was aching and my wrist was aching, my elbows were aching and I said, "You know, I do miss it, but not as much as I thought I did." Maybe I'm just getting too old.'

Three years after filming, the dinosaur museum has continued to go from strength to strength. Tourist numbers have increased and the museum has put on more staff.

'It's grown awfully fast,' David says.

A new section of the museum has opened to the public, called The Dinosaur Canyon Outpost, and scientists are continuing to make discoveries on the grounds. The museum has also taken over the running of the Dinosaur Stampede National Monument – the only known fossilised record of a dinosaur stampede – at Lark Quarry Conservation Park, 110 kilometres south-west of Winton. And David's team of managers and staff has found its most complete sauropod to date – which has been named after Judy.

'It's absolutely beautiful,' David says. 'We have got a whole neck. Judy was happy with it – I think so.'

Farmers in the region are still struggling, but the tourists are helping to bring much-needed income into the community.

Lester Cain shuffles out to the three men sitting on the verandah of his pub.

'You blokes want another beer or something?' he asks.

'Righto, mate.'

From the verandah of the Middleton Hotel, it's dusty, flat country. In the distance are rocky hills which turn golden in the afternoon light.

Middleton. Population: nine. It's pretty close to the middle of nowhere. Lester and his wife, Val, have been here since 2005, but he reckons it's almost time to give the game away.

'I've done me time. Old age is catching up on me,' Lester says. 'Running a pub was very different to what I thought it would be. When I was on the other side of the bar I was a bit of a rat, you know. And I used to say, one day I wouldn't mind having a go at running a bar. When I actually done it, I'd never done it before. It was fairly different to what I imagined it to be.'

He's quite comfortable behind the bar. It's lilac and yellow, with shelves lined with colourful fabric stubby holders, old bottles, some rusted horseshoes and a couple of dusty trophies.

These days, he can't stand drunks.

'Before I came here, the one thing I gave a lot of thought to was that I'd probably end up my best customer,' he says. 'But I quite surprised myself. I drink a lot of tea. People come in and they are always trying to buy me a beer. When mates turn up I always go and make a cup of tea. They say have a beer, and I say, "Oh, I've got a cup of tea now, I'll have a beer later on," and put them off. When you're running a pub you have to be fairly diplomatic. You can't offend too many people. But I surprised myself. I drink very little. I drink less now than I did before. It's just there, and you realise: righto, you've got to have a bit of self-discipline or something.'

Sometimes he has to tell people they've had too much, and he offers them a room. One of a row of five dongas out the back.

'Occasionally I have taken the keys off people. I don't like doing it.'

A road train rumbles past, loaded with cattle.

It's 2015 and *Back Roads* is filming an episode in nearby Winton. The team has made the trip to Middleton to meet Lester, and the crew making a movie right out the front of his pub.

One of the dominant characters in the film *Goldstone*, a sequel to *Mystery Road*, is the vast, open and isolated outback. It's just 'home' to Lester and his wife, Val. But he appreciates what others, such as the movie producers, see in the country.

'There's some spectacular scenery here,' he says. 'I always said, the country just west of here, I always said if John Wayne knew that country was here, he'd come back and make one more movie just for old time's sake.'

His pub looks like the set of a movie. It's an old wooden building with a rusted tin roof, set beside the highway but surrounded by empty land. There's an old stagecoach out the front.

He came out here because his son, Stoney, was getting a lot of work helicopter-mustering in the area. It's remote, but not as isolated as their last property, Swanvale, near Stonehenge, about six hours drive to the south-east. They'd lived there 24 years.

'It doesn't compare to Stonehenge. We never saw anyone. No one ever came in there,' he says. 'Whereas along here, even through the summer, there's always a few travellers poking through. It's not lonely or that. It doesn't really matter much where you live.'

Lester's white hair is tamed by an ageing wide-brimmed hat, and he gets around without shoes. It has its dangers, though. Two years ago he was bitten on the foot by a snake.

'I was on my own here in the summertime. I was running the pub on my own,' he says. 'I was just closing up and a snake hooked me.'

Fortunately, he'd once gone through an induction process to work on the set of an American documentary filmed in the outback about the inland taipan, considered by some to be the most deadly snake in the world. He'd been the camel wrangler on set.

'We were practising getting bitten by a snake and wrapping ourselves up and what to do,' he says. 'And that's what I thought, well, that's what they told you to do, you just wrap it up and don't move. So that's what I did.'

He was taken to Winton, and then flown by the Royal Flying Doctor Service to Mount Isa.

'When I got bitten by the snake, the flying doctor who picked me up, he said to me, "I wouldn't be worried much about an old snakebite, mate. I'd be more worried about your heart," he says.'

So Lester had it checked out, and will soon be flown to Brisbane for surgery. He's pretty pragmatic about it.

'Righto, I've got a heart problem. I fix it or I die,' he says. 'They say you've got a two per cent chance of things going wrong. That's not bad odds, is it, and we've had a pretty good life.'

He's certainly had a varied life. Lester was born in Biloela, west of Gladstone, Queensland, in 1943. He became a ringer as a teenager, and worked and travelled throughout rural Queensland.

'I done it for a fair while, mate,' he says. 'All the mustering was done on horses in those days. We had fairly big camps and it was pretty labour-intensive and pretty slow. Today they are all mechanically mustering. I wouldn't say it was really hard work. We lived kind of rough, though. We slept on the ground and we ate on the ground and we lived on the ground. It certainly wasn't as hard as shearing or fencing. Or swinging an axe. That was pretty hard work.'

He met Val when he was in his early thirties, and when Australia went through a beef slump in the 1970s, when prices crashed, he bought his place Swanvale, near Stonehenge.

He and Val ran cattle and sheep on the 170,000-acre (69,000-hectare) property for 24 years. They have two children, Stoney and Corina.

'We bought country for practically nothing,' he says. 'If the beef slump hadn't have come I'd have worked for wages all my life. Things were cheaper. We got in. Sometimes [with] slumps, if you get on the right bounce they're a great opportunity. Same as buying houses in a slump. You can buy cheap and then within a few years things turn around. It's a gamble but lots of things in life are a gamble. If you pull it off, they say you're smart and if you don't pull it off, they say you're just a mug.'

They sold out in 2003 and moved to Longreach because Lester was having health problems.

'When I was in Longreach, I was buggered,' he says. 'I couldn't do any work or anything much. I had no energy. I used to go away and do a little bit of work, not much, and come back and sleep most of the time.'

The doctors eventually diagnosed him with a cancerous tumour in his nose.

'It took them a couple of years to actually diagnose what was wrong, and they pulled that thing out of me and I felt all right.'

Stoney was in Winton with his helicopter-mustering business, and wanted to move to Middleton. Lester had been to Middleton before. He first came through when he was working as a drover, in about 1961, herding bullocks through town. Just before they bought the pub, he and Val had been through running feral camels off a property called Ethabuka, west of Bedourie. He mustered them on a motorbike.

'We bought them up here and bent them around a bit, and civilised them a bit, and walked them up the road for about 500 kilometres,' he says.

Lester's worked quite a lot with camels over the years. And on film sets. In 2001 he drove camels in a coach for a re-enactment of the early Cobb & Co coach transportation days. In these parts, in the late 1890s, Cobb & Co used camels to pull their coaches, because the water sources were too far apart for horses, he says. Additional boreholes were later added.

'I've done a bit of camel work. We were basically just mustering, running feral camels and sending them to the abattoirs. I've run camels and broken them in and worked them. Camels have a bad name but they're very intelligent and pretty easy.'

He enjoyed the challenge of mustering – of both camels and bullocks. 'It's a bit of an adventure – gives you an adrenalin rush. When you're down in the scrub mustering and you get those big old bullocks that haven't been mustered for eight or ten years, running them is the best thrill you can get with your pants on, as I used to say. You've just got to know what you're doing, and not be in the wrong place at the wrong time. If you do everything right, it runs like clockwork. There's nothing to it.'

Looking back, Lester says he is proudest of those mustering days. 'I've run some pretty big camps in my time and some of those boys that worked for me, they turned out very smart men. I kind of like to think I taught them,' he says.

'In life you never, ever judge a person while everything is going all right. You bide your time and judge people how they come up when everything is going wrong. When I first run a mustering camp an old fella told me that.

'It's pretty true.'

Note: The first part of this chapter is an updated feature story published by *Back Roads* when the episode first aired in 2015.

19

Thallon

Location: Thallon is 534 km south-west of Brisbane in southern Queensland.

Population: 257

Aired: The *Back Roads* episode on Thallon was one of the first episodes in the fourth season in 2018. It was hosted by a guest presenter, news anchor Joe O'Brien.

LEANNE BURGESS MET STUART Brosnan at a barbecue at his parents' house. The first time she saw him, his blonde hair was streaked with blue and red – he was a sight. It didn't matter; they both felt something was right.

'It was a feeling that I'd probably never felt before, yeah, so it was pretty nice,' Stuart recalls. 'It was just like a light bulb moment.'

He'd been working as a wool classer in woolsheds about the place. He had broad shoulders and sun-kissed hair.

'They use what's called "raddle" on sheep when they draft them up after shearing to mark different characteristics and some of that ended up in Stu's hair,' Leanne explains. 'Just people in the woolshed having a bit of fun.'

Leanne, a fresh-faced school teacher with delicate features and brown shoulder-length hair, was at his house when he'd returned home at day's end. It was 1987.

'I was teaching one of Stuart's younger brothers at the time and coincidentally his parents, Pat and Lila, had asked me out for a barbecue,' she says.

Two other teachers, Karen Wool and Robyn Perry, who had been in town a year or so, were also invited.

Like Stuart, Leanne was awestruck. 'We just sort of locked eyes and that was it, which sounds very corny, but it is basically what happened,' Leanne says. 'A couple of days later I actually rang a friend of mine from university and said, "I've met the man I'm going to marry."'

Even though he had blue-and-red hair.

'He was looking fairly scruffy because he'd been in the shed all day and in his shearing clothes and things like that but ... yeah, I can't explain what it was but we just knew.'

Stuart wasn't much of a talker. But the connection was instant. And they were unofficially engaged six weeks later.

'Probably the timing surprised me, but I instantly said yes. I didn't have to think about it,' Leanne says.

Stuart was active in the community. He was president of the Daymar Tennis Club. Leanne had only recently arrived in town. They both kept it a secret.

'We didn't announce it publicly,' Leanne says, laughing. 'He thought I'd change my mind so he didn't want to tell anybody. There were a few eyebrows raised because Stuart was a Catholic and I was Protestant and that was not the done thing and I wasn't going to convert. So it did set tongues talking, I suppose.'

Stuart popped the question after they'd spent a weekend away with the other teachers at Lightning Ridge, a couple of hours drive from Thallon.

'Well, we were planning to get married pretty quickly because that's what you did,' Leanne says. 'We talked to Stu's parents about leasing part of the farm and then in February 1989 Stuart had his accident, so that really changed everything.'

Stuart had grown up 20 kilometres out of Thallon on a sheep property. He was one of eight children, with six brothers and a sister, and went to school in Daymar, another small town nearby.

'Dad, one thing he did teach us was how to work. Started us early, which was not a bad thing,' Stuart says. 'It was mainly sheep. We had a few cattle but not many. But then the wool industry sort of collapsed in the late 1980s, and farming wheat and that grew more and more through the 1980s and 1990s, and they've gone from wool sheep to meat sheep. There's been a fair few changes and they've grown a bit since then too. They've got a bit more country now.'

Leanne had had a similar upbringing. She'd grown up on a property 30 kilometres west of Goondiwindi (about a two-hour drive east of Thallon), but moved into Goondiwindi when her father sold the property in 1980. Thallon was her first teaching posting out of university. She moved into the teachers' house with the two other teachers, Robyn and Karen.

'They'd taught in Thallon for a year already so they had the nice bedrooms in the three-bedroom house and I got the smallest one, which was called the cupboard – tiny.'

It was basic. The water supply was untreated river water, or tank water. And there was a party-line telephone. But Thallon was a lovely place, set on the Moonie River, the 500-kilometre waterway that stretches from Dalby in south-western Queensland into New South Wales. It was vibrant and busy. At harvest time it became the second-biggest wheat depot in Australia. The railway was a hive of activity, with stock and bales of wool going out, replacing the groceries and fuel coming in.

When the other two teachers left at the end of the year, Leanne moved into a caravan provided by the department.

'It was in the corner of the police horse paddock. The education department set up a little fenced area there and put the caravan in,' she says. 'It was lovely. It had a green velour corner lounge and mirror tiles. It was fabulous because it actually had air conditioning and the house didn't. So I was in the lap of luxury there.'

Thallon is a boom or bust type of place. When Leanne moved there it was thriving.

'It's always been a really friendly, pretty town, so I always felt very safe – people were always very welcoming and the kids here are just beautiful country kids; well-mannered, interested in learning, so it was a really nice start to teaching,' she says.

Within a few months she'd met Stuart. They proved to be a good team. Leanne was secretary of the Nindigully B&S Association. Along with the rest of the committee, they organised a huge bachelor and spinster ball together. A thousand people turned up and it raised $10,000 for the ambulance service.

A few months later, as they were planning their wedding, Stuart went away on holiday with friends to a houseboat on the Myall Lakes at Bulahdelah in northern New South Wales. Then an accident – one moment in time – which would change the course of their lives forever.

'I dived off the top of a houseboat into a couple of metres of water but it wasn't deep enough and so I broke my neck,' Stuart says. He doesn't remember much more about that day.

Leanne was in Thallon when she heard the news. She'd stayed behind to work.

'It was the worst day of my life,' she says. 'It was just devastating because we didn't get a lot of details straight away, so that was really hard to cope with, not knowing exactly how bad it was and having him so far away.'

She went to Stuart's parents' property to wait for news. It was about four or five hours before it trickled through: Stuart had been helicoptered to Royal North Shore Hospital's spinal unit in Sydney.

Leanne immediately asked some friends to drive her two hours south across the New South Wales border to Moree where she chartered a plane to Sydney. She was the only one on board, except for the pilot. It all felt like a blur – until the journey took a startling turn.

'I sat up the front with him and we were going over Tamworth and he said would you mind going to the back of the plane and grabbing the thermos so we can have a cup of coffee,' she says. 'I think he was actually trying to distract me because he realised it was a pretty difficult time.

'So I got up very gingerly. It was only a small plane, and I was trying to avoid the controls and the knobs and everything and I put my foot between the two seats and there was some flight manuals and things on the floor there, and I took one more step towards the back of the plane and it just dropped out of the sky. He said get back in the seat, put your seat belt on, and he was trying to work out what had happened.'

The pilot sent a mayday alert to Tamworth Airport. Then he realised the flight manuals had been covering the fuel switch in between the two seats and that Leanne had accidentally flipped the switch to 'off'.

'He turned the fuel back on and we were right,' Leanne says.

She made it to Sydney, and then the taxi dropped her at the wrong end of the Royal North Shore Hospital car park at 2am. Eventually she found her way to Stuart's bedside.

'They were pretty understanding and let me stay as long as I liked for those first few days because it was pretty touch-and-go,' she says. 'I was just sitting there with him doing whatever needed to be done and I think the nurses probably kept me busy to try and distract me.'

Stuart was in the Royal North Shore Hospital for three months.

'They had him on pethidine so he was having some pretty interesting moments,' Leanne says.

Stuart adds, 'I was doing a bit of surfing with the sheepdog and a few things.'

Leanne settled into a routine. After a couple of weeks, one morning she decided not to rush to the hospital – she would be there for the long haul.

'They rang me and said we think he's got a clot on his lung. You need to come up but don't tell him because we don't want to cause him any anxiety because that might make it worse,' Leanne says. 'You need to ring his parents and you need to tell them. So that was a very long day waiting for Stu's mum to fly down so that she could be with us.'

Stuart got through it. And over time, the cloud of pain and confusion dispersed, and he realised where he was. And that Leanne was by his side.

'It was pretty life-changing, really,' he says. 'You know, I think some of the doctors could probably learn a bit more tact or handle things better. It was pretty brutal at the time.'

Leanne was 22, and Stuart was 21. Stuart had a spinal cord injury and was paralysed from the chest down.

'They sort of tried to crush all hope, really, didn't they, right from the word go,' Leanne says. 'It was hard.'

Stuart describes the realisation about his loss of mobility as 'pretty ordinary'.

'You realise pretty early on when you're in there, there's varying degrees. We classified them – another bloke that was in there with me at the time. There were the quads, the paras and the slightly inconvenienced bastards. Some people in there were a lot worse than I am, so you've got to hang onto what you can, I think, to get through. But it's certainly been difficult for us.'

Stuart says he wouldn't have survived without Leanne.

'They tried to tell Leanne that relationships, they don't last after a spinal cord injury and, you know, you're better off getting out now,' Stuart says.

Leanne recalls, 'I started asking, can you please teach me what I'm going to need to do when we go home, and we were actually told that only five per cent of relationships survive after a spinal injury so you're really wasting your time,' Leanne says.

Stuart adds, 'Get out now.'

Leanne says the advice wasn't helpful. 'It wasn't good because we knew that wasn't going to be the case, or we didn't feel that that was going to be the case at that stage,' she says.

Stuart was transferred to a hospital in Brisbane and Leanne started teaching there to be with him. They spent eight months there before moving back to Thallon, to live with Stuart's parents on their property.

It was a relief to leave hospital, if a bit daunting. 'We were still very young so you had that optimism of youth. We weren't looking too far ahead because we weren't sure what to expect. It was just a huge adjustment. He'd been in hospital and people had come to visit, but that was different to going home.'

Slowly, they started looking at how they could adapt to the situation, rather than be shattered by it. 'It was day by day for quite some time because you didn't dare go any further than that – it was hard enough getting through the day, let alone thinking too far ahead,' Leanne says.

They returned to Thallon and lived at the property for about a year to see if they could make it work.

'We knew that being out here you're not going to be able to access the care services,' she says. 'We decided to build a house in Thallon and get married and just charge on regardless.'

The community raised $15,000, which was spent building a swimming pool to help Stuart with his physio and exercise.

They were married in the nearby town of St George on 14 September 1991.

'It was a quiet affair of about 160 people because when you've got a family the size of Stuart's there's a lot of relatives,' Leanne says.

'Neither of us were nervous before the wedding. It was just like let's get married so we can get on with the rest of our lives. Because if Stuart hadn't had his accident we would have been married sooner than that. We just wanted to get married so we could move into our house and start our lives together after what had happened.'

They hadn't really contemplated life anywhere else.

'Never even considered it, no,' Stuart says. 'But we were probably still pretty short-term focused then, like not making grandiose plans or anything.'

Leanne returned to teach at Thallon's school.

'It was about me having a job at the school here, us being surrounded by friends and family at that time, and living in a community that was easy for Stu to be in.'

They built a house that Stuart could easily access, and one of their friends became his carer.

'There were no trained carers out here so she volunteered to do that, which was pretty amazing, which meant that I could have full-time work, and so it worked. You know when you're coping with change of that magnitude you need to keep everything else as familiar as possible, so that, it really helped.'

For Stuart, coming to terms with the reality was a staged process. 'After I got through the angry stage and, you know, feeling sorry for myself a bit, I went back to uni and studied and went from there.'

He did an associate diploma in business accounting.

They stayed in Thallon for eight years, and another two at the family farm, before they decided they needed to move away. They'd been looking for a more moderate climate without the temperature extremes of Thallon.

'The heat and the cold were just getting a bit much because I haven't got the best thermostat,' Stuart says.

Leanne adds, 'We'd go out in winter and Stu would get near the fire bucket but he wouldn't be able to warm up and, you know, the next day, the next morning, he'd still be freezing cold because it's just a part of the injury. And then you go out on a day to the cricket and he'd heat up but he wouldn't realise that he was heating up, and so then it would be icepacks and things to get him to cool down.'

And the memories surrounding them were hard.

'Stuart was just surrounded by all the things that he used to be able to do, and it was hard for him to find a way forward, so we thought we'd move to the beach, as you do,' she says.

At the end of 2001, they moved to a town outside Bundaberg, 700 kilometres away. It was quiet. Next to the beach. With lots of trees.

'We didn't know a soul,' Leanne says.

Stuart became the general manager at a not-for-profit organisation that provides services for people with disabilities. He was soon promoted to chief executive and is now the financial manager, as he can do that role remotely, from home.

Despite moving so far away, the couple have retained a strong connection with Thallon. They have good friends and family there, and are passionate about its survival.

When they left in 2001, Thallon had already begun to decline, with the drought of the 1990s and the scaling back of rail services. Then in 2009 the railway station closed altogether and Thallon also endured a run of floods, followed by droughts. 'Thallon had hit rock-bottom – there'd been a lot of business closures and people were generally frightened that they were going to lose their town,' Leanne says.

In the late 1980s, soon after they'd met, the nearby town of Daymar had gone through a similar experience. It had been a vibrant community but once the school closed, everything else soon followed.

It was weighing on their mind.

'Thallon came perilously close to suffering the same fate really, even though it's a much larger town,' Leanne says.

'If something doesn't happen to halt that decline they just disappear. It's really sad. But I was much more emotional about what was happening with Thallon. Because we'd lived there 15, 16 years. Seeing what was happening and seeing what it used to be compared to what it was becoming was quite emotional.'

In 2010, when the pub was threatened with closure, Leanne got a group together, and they bought it.

'We thought if the pub goes, the whole town goes,' she says. 'The publican had been here for a number of years and he and his wife were getting on, running out of puff, and we were worried that if a town loses its pub, there's no coming back.'

It's become a one-stop shop, and now also includes the post office and a small grocery store.

'Pubs in small towns aren't just pubs. They're the hub of the community. They're where people have christenings and wakes and meet socially. Really important in times of drought, when men off the farms need to get together and try and forget it hasn't rained for six months. Without a pub, a town kind of loses its soul.'

Ask Leanne why she travels 700 kilometres to fight for the town she no longer lives in, she'll say it's the principle.

'I suppose when we first met, Thallon was in its heyday. It was a thriving railway hub. There were lots of kids at the school, you know; there was a shop, post office, a fuel depot – and we had some amazing friends here and had some great memories,' Leanne says. 'It was really vibrant. For us to go away and come back and see it slowly fading away. We just didn't want to let that happen.

'I suppose the people that had stayed here had just got used to seeing everything slowly ebb away, but we had a bit of a different perspective. We thought, well, if we don't give it a go, this would just be really sad. When we visit, we'll be coming back to nothing.'

Stuart says he never really got Thallon out of his system. 'Thallon gave us a lot, so it's probably our turn to pay it back a bit.'

Three years before *Back Roads* visited, and amid another drought, Thallon held a big community meeting to decide on ideas to reinvigorate the town.

'The whole community realised that action was needed,' Leanne says. 'And that we couldn't wait for the council or the state politicians to do something. We had to do something.'

Consultants helped the community come up with nine priorities and developed a plan of action. The Thallon Progress Association arranged for the town's 30-metre-high grain silos to be painted with a giant mural, a strategy that has revitalised other towns, such as Brim in Victoria, where Brisbane artist Guido van Helten painted *Farmer Quartet* on the town's silos. The work forms part of a 'Silo Art Trail' through a number of towns in Victoria's Grampians. Brisbane artists 'The Zookeeper' (Joel Fergie) and 'Drapl' (Travis Vincent) were commissioned to paint Thallon's silos using photos taken by locals. Completed in 2017, the massive artwork shows sheep, the Moonie River and birds against a dramatic pink sunset.

They also brought their own 'big thing' icon – William the endangered northern hairy-nosed wombat – to town.

The silos and big wombat statue have helped boost Thallon's appeal to tourists. And there's even been a few new families move to town.

'There are lots of other members of the community now starting to have a bit more hope and a bit more confidence, so they are starting to step up and do things, Leanne says. 'Just to see the community spirit reignited – that's really what these projects were designed to do, to give people something positive to focus on and events to bring the community together.

'Because that had kind of stopped happening. There wasn't anything to celebrate for a long time. It was just more and more closures and things going wrong, and people got together for funerals and that was about it.'

For Leanne, Thallon is a special community because everyone knows everyone.

'It's just the length of time that we've all known each other, and that continuity of sharing great times together, and sharing, you know, a lot of sadness as well,' she says. 'They're friends, but they're more like family. Stuart and I have such wonderful memories here of when we first met, and every time we come back we make more special memories. So we just want to keep it here, and keep it vibrant, so that we can continue to make new memories in the future.'

20

White Cliffs

Location: White Cliffs is 1022 km west of Sydney.

Population: 148

Aired: *Back Roads* visited White Cliffs in its second season, in 2016.

DICK WAGNER IS TRYING his hand at making a fascinator. It's a pink, purple and blue feather and netting creation. But the hot glue gun is proving a little challenging with his ruddy fingers. There are globs of it everywhere. Little wispy strands hang down off his newly decorated hairclip like a spider's web.

'It's mental health first aid,' he says of the process. 'We just wanted people to unwind, relax and let go of all their cares.'

He puts it on – the bright hairpiece covers his short-cropped, silver-streaked hair. It clashes with his collared blue and white sports shirt. He grins widely.

About a fifth of the town, by Dick's estimate, has turned up for the combined craft workshop in White Cliffs' hall. A fun, free lesson in hat-making. And in basket-weaving. A cacophony of chatter and laughter rumbles around the room as people happily sift through boxes of feathers and flowers. Used coffee cups and material scraps are liberally discarded across the table.

White Cliffs is a creative place. Everyone says so. But whether you've got any discernible talent or not, it's more about being involved. Such is the way of life here, in the remote far west of New South Wales, about three hours drive east of Broken Hill. It's closer to Adelaide than Sydney, and in parts resembles a moonscape, with tens of thousands of old opal mines, some dating back to the earliest prospectors in the early 1890s.

From the surface, it doesn't look like much. Apart from the sky. Sunrise and sunset bring a palette of colour, boldly smeared upwards from the horizon. Most of the homes are below ground, built from old mines. They're called dugouts.

Like many other residents, Dick started as a 'wintery' – someone who visits every winter holidays. They make up about a third of the town. Dick and his wife, Sheryl, and four children started coming on holidays from East Gippsland in rural Victoria in 1985. They loved it so much they'd come back again and again. Eventually they bought a dugout.

'I would have never thought coming up here into the middle of the desert, it would have such an impact,' he says.

'We just fell in love with it – the kids loved it, me personally, this opal bug – I knew it was an itch I had to scratch and when I came here full-time in 2000 to go mining – if I hadn't found an opal, maybe we would have been here for 12 months and would have ended up going back. But I was lucky enough to find opal and it's been one of those things that drives me today.

'I found my opal. I've found my lovely stones. But the community, it's just wonderful. You just want to give back, put back in a little bit, and this is the sort of place you can do that sort of thing. It grows on you. It just bites you.'

Dugouts populate the hills just beyond the main street. Town consists of the hall, sports club, pub and general store.

These days Dick, 70, calls himself a 'married bachelor'.

'There's a lot of us here that are married, but our wives, for various reasons, choose to spend a lot of the year away from White Cliffs,' he says. 'My wife loves it up here but as we have kids and grandkids down south, she prefers to spend a lot of her time down there. We've got our sort of group, I suppose, and if someone needs a hand we'll always pitch in and help each other out.'

When she does visit, Dick says he spends days trying to tidy up the place. But one of the problems with living underground – if not the only one – is the dust.

'I spend the days before she gets here, I clean all the mirrors and do all the dusting and washing and polishing and the first thing she does when she gets here, she cleans all the mirrors and does all the dusting and polishing. Obviously I've got a long way to go. I'm still only an apprentice in that department.'

Dick's dugout is on Turleys Hill, attached to an opal store. It's quite homely and rustic. In the kitchen, there's a pot of soup on the stove and a dozen eggs on the bench. The cupboards are yellow and white. A green oven mitt hangs on a hook on the wall beside a collection of electrical cords leading to downlights around the room. In much of the house the walls are jagged, raw rock. You can see where the rooms have been chiselled out.

One of Dick's favourite features is the en suite attached to the main bedroom. It has a brightly painted aquatic theme, with schools of fish and other marine life swimming the length of the walls around behind the toilet and bath, and the basin mirror.

'There's only a few dugouts in White Cliffs that actually have the en suite attached to the main bedroom,' he says. 'We were lucky. With dugout living, you turn the light out of a night and it's just so black and so quiet. Having an en suite means you don't have to walk through the dugout – in the dark the walls are very unforgiving.'

There is a lot to be said for living underground, especially when the outside temperature gauge is stuck around a sweltering 40 degrees Celsius – or higher. Three metres beneath the red earth of White Cliffs in the dugouts it's a moderate 22 degrees year round.

'Summertime it gets a bit warm up here and we don't have any air conditioning,' Dick says. 'Wintertime, yeah, it doesn't get all that cold. But we don't have any heating. It's so quiet and peaceful for sleeping. World War Three could start outside and you wouldn't know. You're in your own little world here and it's just great.'

Importantly, according to Dick, there are no windows to clean. Though it does require regular maintenance.

'It's sort of like painting and doing your guttering and that at a normal house,' he says. 'You have always got a little bit of an ongoing thing with cracking, and you just get enamel gap filler and a bit of good paint and it's good.

'I have a new kitchen to go in here – or a new second-hand kitchen. I've had it for probably about ten or eleven years – my wife keeps mentioning it but I've resisted the urge so far – it's sitting out the back in one of the rooms out here. There's too much mining to do and too much golf to play – other important things.'

Dick spends a lot of time on his vegetable patch – above ground. It's abundant, full of kale, parsnip, a couple of different types of parsley, plus basil and strawberries.

'People go, oh, you're a vegetarian and I say, no, I'm a vegaholic – love my meat, love my T-bone down the shop every Friday night, but the soup I'm cooking at the moment – and I've just counted up – it's got eight vegies in it. That, to me, that's sort of about the minimum that I like on my plate of a night.'

Many of the dugouts have been burrowed through the remnants of the early mines. Perhaps the most remarkable one in town belongs to couple Cree Marshall and Lindsay White. It glows white, with expert finishes, as the hall snakes around through archways and across intricate designs of cut tile on the floor.

Cree is an artist. She is vibrant, with a shock of bright red hair, cut short to frame her pale face. Lindsay has short thick grey hair. He is now a builder, and is tall and broad-shouldered.

Cree's art hangs on the wall, and is felt in every room.

'I think it's probably the only place in White Cliffs that's fully rendered in the walls, which means we were able to paint them white, so there's a lot of light reflecting through them,' she says. 'I think it's peaceful too. The dugouts are all so different and they all have their own unique personalities.'

Cree moved to the town from Sydney in 1992 in search of artistic inspiration. Originally from New Zealand, she worked as a graphic artist before moving into interior design. She wanted to do some creative writing, and her cousin in Sydney owned a place here, and said she could live here for free while she pursued the craft.

'I drove into town and I took one look around and thought, this has got to be the ugliest place I have seen,' she says. 'And when I walked into the dugout for the first time I thought, hmm, I'm either going to love this place or hate it.

'But then I've got to say, the first night coming on sunset I went out for a walk, just walking around the land. I don't think I'd ever recognised before how powerful this land is. It's so old, and it's so powerful. I think you can feel that. It seeps into your bones and I thought, okay, I'm going to love this place. It's a good place to be creative in any way that you want to, really. It gives you the space. Anything that requires you to be solitary, I think.'

The dugout was small and basic. There was no electricity or hot water, and an outside toilet. It was through that dugout she met her future partner, Lindsay, with whom many years later she would build the incredible underground home they both now live in.

Lindsay's been in White Cliffs since the 1960s. For more than 50 years. He was working as a wool classer and called into town to get a soft drink one weekend. And stayed.

'I had to pull my car up between the hotel and the shop, and there was a little kid having a crap in the middle of the road,' he recalls. 'So I waited for him to finish. A bloke come out of the store, grabbed him by the scruff of the neck with half a poo still hanging out of him and carted him back into the store. So that was my welcome to White Cliffs. I went into the shop saying how damn hot it was, because it was over 50 degrees, and I met a lady in there.'

She was an artist and owned an underground art gallery in one of the hills, and she invited Lindsay to take a look and cool off.

'I walked in there, couldn't believe it,' he says. 'It was just amazing. It was cool. It blew me away. I said, how do you get one of these? They said put four pegs in the hill anywhere you like and just start digging. I borrowed a pick and shovel and a wheelbarrow and every weekend I'd come into White Cliffs and build my first dugout.'

It took three years to finish. When he finishes working on his masterpiece – their current home – he'll have built five dugouts.

'When I finish this one, that will be the last,' he says.

Lindsay's first dugout all those years ago was also a huge improvement on other underground homes.

'When I built the first one, I put a few modern things in and it really got the rest of the town a little bit amazed that you could have carpet or you could have concrete or you could have electric light in dugouts – and running water and showers and toilets underground,' he says. 'It really got the whole place going.

'We just try to create something, that's all. When people come in they go, oh, I can do that, that's terrific. And it's great because that inspires people.'

He says there's something comforting about living underground: 'You feel secure and you're surrounded by nature. White Cliffs is such a fascinating place. There's no police, no mayor. You can build what you like, there's no building plans or permits. People here were so bloody creative. Everyone's dugout is a part of them. The things that they used to build them with: anything they could scrounge, car bonnets and old bits of tin; anything.

'Nowadays things have changed. People are updating. They had earth floors, now they've got concrete floors. They've got lighting, but it was all just amazing the way people created them.'

It was a dugout that eventually brought Lindsay and Cree together in the 1990s.

'I went past this dugout to show some friends, because it was a double-storey dugout where Cree was staying, and not knowing that anybody was there,' he says. 'This was one of the first dugouts that was built. And then this woman appears.'

They started talking.

'She didn't have running water. I went across and did a few jobs. And the next thing we're building dugouts for her.'

Like most people in town, Lindsay isn't averse to looking for a bit of opal. He's come across some digging out some of the houses he's built.

'I've been having a look for an opal just about most of my life and every now and then I get lucky and I trip over one,' he says. 'In this house here, there's a lot I've covered up because if I'd gone mining I'd never have got the house finished. It's in the wall so that's my wall safe.'

The dugouts aren't owned outright but leased via licences from the New South Wales government. For some, there's a cloud over the future of their homes after a successful native title claim spanning a large part of the region.

Dick Wagner fears the licence issue could take many more years to resolve. He says it's been quite stressful for many people in town. Hence the need for the distraction of a basket-weaving and hat-making workshop. And some 'mental first aid'.

'It's more so that it's a bit of relief for the people to come here and be able to just take five minutes out from not having this debacle going on in the background,' he says. 'To laugh and chuckle, make a hat, make a basket and try and forget all about your troubles and worries.'

Besides, Melbourne Cup is just around the corner. In six months' time. Preparation is required.

'We have fashions on the opal fields here on Melbourne Cup day,' Dick explains. 'Usually you get dressed up in your best suit. I decided to get dressed up and wear a fascinator last year, and I enjoyed that.'

This year, he'll have two, freshly created by his own hand. 'I could wear both,' he smiles. 'One on each side of the head.'

21

Corryong

Location: 442 km north-east of Melbourne, close to
the New South Wales border and Mount Kosciuszko
National Park.

Population: 1348

Aired: The episode on Corryong was the first in *Back Roads'*
third series. It first aired on 27 November 2017.

And the Snowy River riders on the mountains make
   their home,
Where the river runs those giant hills between;
I have seen full many horsemen since I first commenced
   to roam,
But nowhere yet such horsemen have I seen.

From 'The Man from Snowy River', AB 'Banjo' Paterson.

A HEADLESS SNAKE IS still lying on Joan Sinclair's white gravel front porch a few days after its death. The 83-year-old hit it with a shovel to stop it entering her house. Or worse, killing her dog.

'I splattered the poor bugger all over the place,' she says. 'It's not as bad as hitting them with the whipper snipper, I can tell you that much. He came around the corner. I was minding my own business. I said, woah! There was bits of snake flew up the woodshed and all over me. Oh gawd.'

Of course, killing snakes is illegal unless they're an immediate threat to life, but Joan reckons she's on pretty safe ground there.

And she'd know. She's accumulated a lifetime of knowledge about the bush and all its inhabitants in her eight decades at Dargalls, her family property in the foothills of the Snowy Mountains, on the border between New South Wales and Victoria.

It's wild country, both in reality and folklore. Straw-coloured paddocks rise and fall over gentle hills across the rich dairy- and beef-farming region. Beyond, dark-green forested mountains rise, range upon range. Full of promise. The country is described in Banjo Paterson's iconic 1890 poem 'The Man from Snowy River', about a horseman who makes a treacherous chase after a prized colt that's joined the brumbies in inaccessible mountain country and singlehandedly brings him back.

Nearby Corryong has taken ownership of the fable, with a Man from Snowy River Museum and an annual festival.

'I'd better be careful what I say,' Joan laughs heartily. '"Alone and unassisted brought them back" – I mean, that's all hooey. But anyway, I think Banjo had a very romantic, talented mind, but there are more people that don't know how hard it is to get a brumby home than the ones that do.'

Joan, you see, is one of those who do. She's one of Australia's most enduring horsewomen.

Joan's strawberry-blonde hair is tied back in a long plait down her back. A fringe and wisps of hair frame her age-crinkled face, and she wears clear framed glasses that turn dark in the sunshine. She has a glint in her brown eyes. She's wearing a bright blue work shirt, faded jeans and black boots.

In person, Joan is pragmatic and her honesty refreshing. A white sticker on the window of her house encapsulates it best: 'DULL WOMEN HAVE IMMACULATE HOMES'.

'I don't like housework, but I do it because I don't like rubbish and things laying about,' she offers.

She spends most of her time painting the fences, cutting the lawns and working in her garden.

Joan's been living in this house since she was an infant.

'I came here when I was six weeks old and I've had two husbands, and they've both come here,' she says. 'They've both died on me, but that's what happens.'

She doesn't take too much notice of what others think. If she'd listened to them, she would have quit riding decades ago.

'They started that when I was about 60; they were crying about me riding but I don't take too much notice of people,' she says.

Besides, riding beats walking.

'I'm not a walker,' she comments. 'Riding is only half the effort of walking. I'll ride while ever I can. I don't think about it. I rode 25 or so kilometres the other day. It was only the last half a mile I was thinking I'll be glad to get back to the camp. I'm very comfortable in the saddle.'

Her current horse is a chestnut called Yarramin. She also refers to him as 'the big fella'. Back when Joan was a young girl, horses were still the main form of transport available.

She was the youngest of six, with three brothers and two sisters. Her father, Ernie Boardman, was with the forestry department, which was trying to access the mountains to mill the mountain ash trees.

'Everything was done with draught horses. And Dad looked after the horses.'

The forestry workers built an access road and her father camped out with the crew. Joan's mother, Grace, stayed in Tumut with the children until her father bought the property she's still living in. It was 1935 when they all moved in.

'These paddocks were all bush. Dad and my brothers cleared all this country.

'There were always horses around the place,' she says.

Her father would carry her in the saddle when she was just a baby. 'Gosh, I was only a little fella,' she recalls.

When she was old enough, she attended school in Towong. Joan says it was a 14-mile (22.5-kilometre) horse ride each way, through two rivers.

'Sometimes the water was up to your saddles; you had to cross your legs or you would have wet boots,' Joan says. 'Sometimes it wasn't that high. It was good.'

Joan used to go along with Ernie when he took their cattle up into the mountains. 'It's a different world when you get up the bush,' she says.

The family's been farming beef her whole life. Today she has a herd of around 100 Hereford calves in the front paddock.

'That's my form of retirement, the steers. I don't have any females, so if you don't have females about, you don't have trouble,' she says. 'There's no cows, no bulls; you just buy them and everything's done. Pour a bit of drench on them and sit on the verandah and watch them grow. I take great pride in my cattle and I like topping the market. Not just for the money; for the showing off,' she smiles.

She also has two border collies, Emma and Dukes. A cat. Six horses, plus eight visiting brumbies. And a few more horses belonging to a neighbour. And birds.

'I like birds,' Joan says. 'If a bird gets run over or hit by a car, they'll bring it to me. So that's how I started off.'

She has around 50 birds, of different sizes and varieties, in a large aviary in her backyard. Some she's cared for since they were injured. Others she's bought herself. She's taught one or two of them to talk.

Her real passion, though, is horses. Joan's home is full of horse memorabilia. Statuettes of boots and horses. Photos of Joan leading a parade of horses down the main street of Corryong. The front door has a gold horse's head for a doorknocker.

When she was four or five she learned to ride on a goat named David. Though she wouldn't recommend it: 'They're not good to ride ... I only rode him for showing-off purposes.

He had quite big horns and he used to [put his head back] and he'd hit you in the ribs.'

As a precaution, the children would cover David's horns with the rubber ends of a bike's handlebars: 'Then when he hit you in the ribs it wasn't so bad.'

She rode her first horse, Tatters, from the age of five or six. 'She must have been very dependable because I rode her for a long time,' she says. 'And then she had a foal, called Jewel, a grey one. She was a wonderful polocrosse horse.'

Her favourite horse was a white gelding called Bobby. 'I dearly loved Bobby. He was my trail-riding horse until he got too old. We went a long, long way, rode a lot of mountains together, Bobby and I.'

She's learned a thing or two about horses. And thinks there's some good life lessons in there too.

'Horses, they're individuals,' she says, 'and they are very forgiving. Some people treat horses in such a bad way and they still keep carrying them. My saying is, there's generally only one thing wrong with a horse and that's the bloke that owns it.'

She gestures to her horses in the adjacent paddock. 'These fellows are my mates and they're a lot less trouble than men.'

Growing up, Joan's father would break in horses for extra money. 'He'd break them into the saddle and then he'd break them into the harness,' she says. 'There's an art to breaking in a horse.'

Her father and brothers also went to the local rodeos, as buckjump riders.

'I got on once and got pelted to buggery so I thought, this is not for me. I didn't enjoy it,' she says.

The family had been living on the remote property for about 15 years when the Snowy Hydro Scheme started, opening up the surrounding wilderness. Theirs was one of the last to get a road past it. It came in the 1950s.

It also brought her a fella – Joe Blyton.

'My first husband, he came here with the Snowy Hydro Scheme. He came over to relieve a fellow on holidays for three weeks and I found him and the poor bugger never got away,' she says. 'So he was brought here. He said I'll get a Snowy house and I said, I'm not going to live in a town with people. So we just built a bit more on the house and we lived here with Mum and Dad.'

They had two children, a son, Ron, and daughter, Susan.

Joan used to play polocrosse, ride racehorses and competed in showjumping, but she gave it all up when she married Joe in 1960.

'I used to do anything most that you could do on a horse,' she says.

'I had showjumping horses when I married him. He was a nice man but he was very possessive and once the wedding ring went on I was his.'

She never returned to any of it.

'We were married nearly 30 years when he died. That's a long time to be away from something,' she says. 'You need a lot of wind and a lot of strength to ride over fences and to play polocrosse. And you're also not as brave as you get older.'

She always had horses on the property, though. 'I always made sure the kids had a horse,' she says.

Her son, Ron, had a Shetland stallion called Uncle, and Susan had a black showjumping mare called Kelly.

'Oh, dear God. Uncle was something to behold,' she chuckles. 'Uncle used to throw the chooks about. He'd pick them up anywhere he could get a grip of them. He didn't care where he got them. And the cow. We had a jersey cow we used to milk for the house, and he bit her behind the ear.'

Ron lives in Albury now, but has a business in Corryong, and Joan sees him regularly.

Susan was a budding hairdresser with her own shop in Corryong when she was tragically killed in a car accident at Bringenbrong, about 20 kilometres to the north-west. She was 21. Joan has a large photo of Susan on her wall.

'My children are certainly the most important thing in my life. But I suppose most mothers probably say that. To me, they were my achievement, I think.'

After 30 years of marriage, Joe died from cancer.

'I kicked the grass and swore and said I'd never get married again, but then I was silly enough to do it again,' she says.

'I married Frank and I said if you want me, you come here. And so we were married for 14 years and he died with cancer.

'So I've given up this marrying business.'

She reckons she's gained an insight or two about human behaviour from the horses. She's currently got a herd of brumbies in a bottom paddock.

'There's a stallion here and the brumby stallion and he were fighting and carrying on for six months,' she says. 'They were tormenting our horses and kept chasing them away.

'Anyway, about three weeks ago he came up and there was a row, so I went and opened the gate. I got eight of the brumbies. So they are out there now. They are shut in my paddock, but they can't get to those other horses. They're just typical males. They have more sense than man. I like men but, God, they're a nuisance. Then, brumbies can be a nuisance too.'

She says it is comforting to live in the same house all these years.

'I've been all over the world. It's lovely to have been to London and Paris and Rome and Cape Town and everywhere, but, by God, it's good to get home.'

Her horses too have brought her joy.

'It's given me great comfort, really, because you always feel there's a friend there. You always feel that if you've got a good horse, got a good dog, you always feel you've got a mate.'

22

Queenstown

Location: Queenstown is 260 km north-west of Hobart, in Tasmania.

Population: 1790

Aired: *Back Roads* visited Queenstown in late 2015. The episode first aired in January 2016. It was the final episode in the first series of the show.

ANTHONY COULSEN IS PEERING over the side of an old Huon pine bridge near a disused railway line. There's a wide, tannin-stained river rushing about ten metres below. He's lean with blond hair, and dressed for adventure in a fluorescent jacket.

With a gentle swing of his right arm, he lowers a billy can down over the side. It's tied to a rope which rapidly unfurls, like a bungee jumper's cord. Within seconds the can is enveloped in water, and he scoops it back up effortlessly. He's done it so many times before that he doesn't spill a drop.

'It doesn't get better than this, not in my mind, anyway,' he says.

Once boiled, the water of the Bird River, in the heart of western Tasmania's wilderness, is the perfect base for Anthony's tea. Aside from the river water, the brew is made out of the leaves of the tall, skinny sassafras tree, which is in plentiful supply here. And like everything else, there's a story behind it.

'The guys who built this railway track back in 1898 loved tea,' he says, pouring a cup. 'Tea was the thing and it was pretty hard to get down here. So they used the tea leaves two and three times over, and on the second and third time they were getting a bit bland so they added some sassafras leaves to the tea water. We sweeten ours with local leatherwood honey. Taste it and see what you think. It should taste like the forests around us.'

It does. The surrounding landscape is a patchwork of different shades of green. Bright mosses cling to the bridge path. Tall ferns clump together and form a canopy, mingled with Huon pines. Birds call out to each other, competing to be heard over the river.

The wilderness has reclaimed this place. A busy railway cut through it 120 years ago, lugging copper out from Crotty, an old mining town now inundated by modern Lake Burbury, about 45 kilometres to the north near Queenstown, to be loaded onto ships for market.

The nearby port town of East Pillinger once boasted a population of 600, with 80 homes and three hotels. Even a

Catholic church. But its fortunes were tied closely to the North Mount Lyell Company it was created to serve, and when that melded into the region's major resource company, the Mount Lyell Mining and Railway Company, the infrastructure at East Pillinger was no longer needed.

It's a familiar story in these parts. The western region of Tasmania has long been shaped by the rising and falling fortunes of the mines and industry. Boom times have come, to be replaced with periods of pain, even sadness, and uncertainty. Some towns, like East Pillinger, couldn't survive and have been folded back into the forest, quiet except for the birdsong and the occasional passing of curious bushwalkers.

Others, like Queenstown, are fighting back. When *Back Roads* visited in 2015, Queenstown was defiantly holding on. The Mount Lyell copper mine – until then Australia's longest continually operating mining field – had been placed in 'care and maintenance' mode two years earlier following two tragedies in which three workers had been killed. Hundreds lost their jobs, and many left town. Those who hadn't left already were digging in.

Anthony was born and bred in Queenstown, into a mining family.

Of course, you couldn't get a greater contrast to the greenery here than Queenstown. The river is still a polluted tinge of orange. The town is surrounded by slowly revegetating bald mountains, stripped bare by industry over the generations.

But they too hold a rugged beauty. The mountains' colours change in the afternoon light as Queenstown lives on to fight another day.

'One of the big tourism drawcards was the lunar landscape, or the denuded landscape, of Queenstown, which was certainly true up until I'd say the early–mid-1980s,' Anthony says. 'I grew up in the '70s and we had a hell of a time playing among relics and mine ruins, which, when you're a kid, you don't think that much about. But it did register somewhere in there that, hey, something big has happened here long ago.'

He started researching the old mines and now goes on exploring adventures with his son, Aaron, to discover their remains.

'Then we'll go and research that and find out what it was all about so that we can potentially offer it to tourism – it's a great pastime, lots of fun and we're making it our profession,' he says.

Anthony's grandfather and father had worked in the mining industry. And when he left school, he joined the Mount Lyell mine too.

'I started in 1984 at 15 years old as a first-year apprentice – one of 100 apprentices at Mount Lyell,' Anthony says. 'That was what you did. You had really two options – to move out and become academic and some kind of career professional, or off to the mines, my boy, and that's just what I did. But seriously, 15 years old – you're a kid. Who knows what you're going to do. So I just went to work.'

These days he's a tour guide. He brings tourists on adventures to explore Tasmania's wild and rugged country.

Anthony has been coming to this patch, at Bird River, since he was a little boy. Back then it would take him three days to reach Pillinger and return to Queenstown.

'I experienced this when I was young and it's taken me,' he says. 'It's my favourite place on the planet. Generations to come need to have this. So it's well worth the conservation. What I'm doing with tourism is all about conservation.'

The area now forms part of Tasmania's 1.5-million-hectare Wilderness World Heritage Area. It has for decades. But it very nearly wasn't protected. The World Heritage Area encompasses the nearby Gordon and Franklin rivers, which were at the heart of one of Australia's most significant – and divisive – environmental battles back in the early 1980s.

Tasmania's Hydro-Electric Commission (HEC) proposal to build a dam, which would have resulted in the inundation of vast stretches of the wild rivers, galvanised the Australian public. It led to the largest mass civil disobedience campaign in Australian history, led by Bob Brown, then the head of the Tasmanian Wilderness Society, with hundreds chaining themselves to the HEC compound or blocking the river in dinghies at Warner's Landing. Thousands were arrested, including Bob Brown himself.

Back in Queenstown, however, the locals were vehemently supportive of the hydro scheme. It meant jobs.

Anthony says that 30 years ago at the height of the dams blockade – as the locals called it – he would never have spoken openly in favour of conservation. But now it's his life.

'Queenstown was pro-dam – almost everyone was pro-dam,' he says. 'At that young age you're not going to speak up against Mum and Dad, uncles and aunts – but now, yeah, I'd chain myself to that tree if they were going to destroy this.'

Anthony kept his green feelings hidden for much of his adult life. But they were bubbling away below the surface. He was still plugging away at Queenstown's copper mine, but growing increasingly unhappy. He was stuck in an internal battle with himself.

In 1994, after 101 years of activity, the Mount Lyell Mining and Railway Company ceased operations. The mine lease has changed hands a couple of times. The culture of the mine, and the town, changed, and the town's reputation as a rough place grew.

'You had to have a real reason to go there and it's not a thoroughfare to and from anywhere either, so no one had to go there.'

By 2009 Anthony had had enough of the workplace culture, and the modern mine. 'I needed to do something else,' he says. 'I was miserable. I'd seen some success in the job but I couldn't do it any more.'

A different career beckoned. In tourism. And the wilderness he'd visited as a kid. So when the man running the tours of the historic Mount Lyell mine announced he was going to retire, Anthony seized the opportunity to take over.

'Opportunity knocked so I jumped pretty abruptly from working in the mining industry to the tourism and hospitality industry,' he says.

It was a big step, and a stressful time. Anthony says he felt a weight off his shoulders when he walked out the project manager's door, having resigned.

'It was a sense of relief but there was a little bit of, oh, my gosh, what did I just do, what am I going to do now?' he says. 'But January 2010, when I did my first tour and it was successful, it was onward and upward after that.'

Mining tourism was the biggest drawcard for tourists to Queenstown at that stage, and Anthony soon found himself back at the mine, showing tourists around his former workplace.

From the get-go, though, he yearned for the vast, mysterious wilderness and wanted to show it off to tourists. From the relic-strewn sites from pioneering days to the hydropower developments and the magnificent wild rivers.

As the mine's fortunes fluctuated, Anthony and his partner Joy Chappell, diversified. By 2011, he was showing tourists around the World Heritage Area.

'In hindsight it's the best thing I ever did,' he says. 'At the time it was quite daunting. But it was only a matter of months until I felt this was rocking my world. This was great.

'The first tour into the wilderness was the big turning point because then we'd started to get diverse and get away from the mine tour. It's driven us into a different space. It's been hard work. It's been a big change.'

Now, instead of the mines, the tours celebrate the World Heritage listing and the controversial battle over the Gordon-below-Franklin Dam project.

In many ways, Anthony's come full circle. He's been bringing his own son, Aaron, to Bird River. Aaron calls it 'the Dark Forest', and sees himself and dad Anthony as the Defenders of the Wilderness.

'I probably come here more than anybody, I'd imagine,' Anthony says. 'It's just the natural beauty and the fact that you feel a little bit protective sometimes. You feel responsible. I feel responsible for demonstrating it, showing it off, interpreting it properly. But protecting it.'

Anthony describes the patch of land, just inside the World Heritage-listed park as 'one of the best-kept secrets in tourism'. But after *Back Roads'* visit, the secret was out. He is forever enthusiastic about the tourism potential of Queenstown, particularly with the reopening of the West Coast Wilderness Railway, which draws visitors and transports them in time along a recreated 1890s passage through the rainforest.

'That's given us a central iconic attraction, a bit like Cradle Mountain, Port Arthur, if you like – or Gordon River,' Anthony explains. 'We can potentially see 140, perhaps more, people a day move on and off that train – which is a wonderful thing, but again it's just more than mining heritage. It's part of a bigger story.'

It's now 2018, and in the three years since *Back Roads* visited, Anthony believes the town is starting to bounce back from the mine's shift in operations to 'care and maintenance' mode. It's beginning to embrace a new future, led by tourism.

'People think differently now,' he says. 'It's not all about mining per se. Although it's still a big thing for us, of course, and everyone wants to see it go ahead. But it's not imperative any more. The place will survive, with or without it.'

He guesses about 60 per cent of the population in town has been there for less than five years. New tourism ventures have started. Hotels are being refurbished. Anthony and Joy have bought the Art Deco Paragon Theatre, and have added historic hydropower station tours to their suite of offerings. But the biggest shift has been the emphasis on the wilderness rather than the mines.

'I wouldn't say it's an empire,' he says. 'We are working hard, is what we are doing. We had to get pretty diverse. We just got clobbered by the dependence on mining here. We've got right away from that. Around the whole place, there's a bit of a renaissance. It's reinvented itself. 'If the mine opens again then that's great because it will contribute to the economy, but there's a future here without it.'

23

Dunalley

Location: Dunalley is 56 km east of Hobart, in Tasmania.

Population: 316

Aired: *Back Roads* visited Dunalley, in Tasmania, in its third season. The episode aired in December 2017.

SHANE NEVITT ISN'T HAPPY. He lifts the white sheet, revealing a huge, light-pink-coloured pumpkin, propped awkwardly on a white groundsheet.

'She's one of the craziest pumpkins I've ever grown,' he says, frowning. 'She's given us a lot of problems.'

The pumpkin is 85 days old. It's due to be harvested in five days time. Just in time for the 2017 Bream Creek Show, an iconic century-old country fair in Tasmania's south-east.

Shane and his daughters, Bella and Jess, have won their categories in the heaviest pumpkin competition at the show for the past few years. Except for last year. 2016 was a nightmare season. And this one isn't looking much better.

With each victory they've gained knowledge, leading to bigger pumpkins. There's a lot riding on them gaining a new personal best weight, to push them forward towards even greater weights.

'It's a long journey,' Shane says. 'You have the highs and the lows and there's no better feeling. If you can fight with nature and get all the way through with all the winds and survive and nurture your plant, to get through all that pressure over the six months of growing, you harvest it and take it to the show, and that pumpkin hits the scales and you see those magical numbers come up, it's just one big rush. And when we drive off together in the 4WD ute, we are all looking at each other and thinking wow, here we go.'

The only problem is, this year, things haven't exactly gone to plan.

'I don't think we'll win this year,' Shane says. 'This is one of the smallest fruits we've grown. We need to address those problems for next season. And hopefully we'll get back to having the size and the weights of those fruits we hit a bit earlier.'

It's March 2017 and *Back Roads* is filming an episode in the nearby town of Dunalley, about how the local community banded together and rebuilt after devastating bushfires in 2013.

The Bream Creek Show has been a consistent factor throughout the effort, giving the community a chance to come together and have a bit of fun.

Likewise, for many, keeping a vegie patch is a way of relaxing. A place to potter around. Get the hands dirty. And hopefully grow something. But for the Newitts, the backyard of their home in nearby Sorell has become something resembling a finely-tuned military operation. It's serious. And it's scientific. Such is the highly competitive world of Atlantic Giant Pumpkin growing.

'Every day you fight to survive,' Shane says. They've lost seven other pumpkins this season, you see, due to factors beyond their control. The girls have named their last surviving pumpkin the Terminator. They've named all their competition pumpkins since they took up the hobby seven years ago. There's been Big Ben, Big Momma, Maximus, Big Bessie, Optimus Prime.

'I believe she should have been called Funky because she's been a bit difficult for me to grow,' Shane says. 'It's not the sort of pumpkin I usually grow. It's a bit of an odd shape.'

The Terminator has kind of grown back over itself.

'You could never measure her correctly because of all the funny shapes she was taking as she developed,' he says.

The misshapen Terminator squats under a large blue and white tent in the centre of the backyard. The structure is surrounded by a sea of dark-green pumpkin leaves.

The Newitt family have taken extraordinary precautions to protect her from the wind, the cold, the heat.

There's even a small concrete statue of a pug dog with its tongue hanging out, which is standing guard. If there's any movement near the pumpkin he lets out a tinny burst of synthetic barking.

There are also three radios stationed around the yard. One is playing the BBC international news. Another, propped on a wooden stand, is blasting Marvin Gaye's 'Sexual Healing' over the masses of leaves. A plastic thermometer hangs from a piece of wire nearby. They're all necessary and important tools.

'The girls tend go a bit wild and play crazy music to them which is maybe the reason this pumpkin started lurching all over the pad that she grows on,' says Shane. 'People don't realise why we do this. They all think it's lovely because we play music to the plants.

'It's for game. It's for mice, rats, birds. One morning when we woke up, there was this great big bird sitting on top of one of my prized pumpkins. When the bird flew off there was this tiny little scratch mark on the pumpkin. Do you know, that tiny little scratch, it turned into a canyon. The pumpkin fell apart. So with a lot of noise and different frequencies and channels going, they think there's people around.'

Shane is still troubled by last year's wipe-out season, when he lost a giant pumpkin he believes would have been a new Australian record. It was on track to reach a whopping 850 kilos.

'I had it to 585 kilograms at only 46 days, so she was a baby,' he says. 'We had a 40-degree day; the fruit overheated, the plant overheated and it simply aborted. Two months before the show, when we were due to have the weigh-off, it stopped growing and would never have kept that long.'

It was a devastating blow for Shane and the girls. But they tried to take lessons from the experience.

'We tried to cool it down,' he says. 'We tried everything as growers. We tried all sorts of things. It did put us back to the drawing board as to how can we combat this in the future if these sort of things pop up.'

They've now increased the protection for the pumpkins, adding a layer of hessian to the steel-and-sheet tent structure shading the giant fruit.

'What was happening was the steel supports that hold the hoops up were conducting too much heat and it was radiating back at the plants and the fruit,' he says.

Wind can also be a problem.

'Sorell is the home of the wind,' Shane says. 'We can have six months of wind here and it can blow up to 140 kilometres per hour for days and days or weeks and months on end.'

And when it gets cold, Shane uses heat cables to warm the soil underground to a pleasant 23 degrees. Plus there's thick army blankets on hand if it's particularly cold. It's like an electric blanket.

'The pumpkin roots are warm; they love it,' he says.

'It's like us laying back somewhere on a nice, warm beach. And the roots react to the warmth and there you go. We put blankets on the pumpkins too. During the summer, even though we might have a 30-degree day, Sorell or Tassie might be fickle with the weather, we might have a four-degree night. So if that fruit cools off too much, it slows down.'

Shane says people might think there's a certain mystique about growing giant pumpkins. But for him it's straightforward. It's science. The soil is tested repeatedly. There's even tissue samples taken from the leaves.

'It's all precision farming' Shane says. 'It's knowing how to understand the soil and look inside the soil to improve the fertility and you can grow anything. We send a lot of tests off to the laboratory and when the results come back, it's knowing how to amend these figures with nice, natural products that are going to increase the health of the soil.'

He's well aware that some might consider his focused approach to the contest a little extreme.

'We push so far we border between perfection and toxicity. That's how much we push it. We push the envelope so much.'

Shane's family has been farming cattle, sheep and crops in these parts for around 200 years.

'I come from a long line of farmers or primary producers – they've all been in agriculture and farming since we settled here,' he says.

After finishing school, Shane attended the Burnie Agricultural College in the north of the state, and worked most of his life with his father on a cattle-fattening and cropping property. In the past few years he's taken a step back from farming to look after his girls.

'Of course, where we are at Sorell, it's super-rich and some of the best fattening country in this state of Tassie,' he says.

The pumpkins came about, in part, because Shane hopes that one day his girls will be working the land with him or caretakers of their own properties. Bella and Jess started growing pumpkins when they were only four and five years old. That was seven years ago.

'The girls got me into it,' Shane says. 'They started growing first. And what happened was, they asked me, "Dad, we want to grow them heavier and bigger. Can you help us?"

'And that was my way, I suppose, of using these pumpkins sneakily as a tool to convey my growing knowledge to the girls in the hope that one day one or both of them would become primary producers.'

The girls spotted the giant pumpkin competition at the show and were hooked.

'They've always grown vegies since they were three or four years of age,' he says. 'I think with the giant pumpkins they never get bored.'

In 2015, the girls became the Australian junior record holders. Their first pumpkin starting out weighed 56 kilograms. The next year it grew to 132 kilograms, then 260 kilograms and the record-grabbing 362 kilograms.

Shane raises the girls as a single parent for four days of the week.

'It's really pulled us together. It's something we enjoy doing. It's brought everyone together.'

For Shane, it's about spending time with his girls – and competing against his own personal best weights. Though he'd like to claim the Australian record one day. In 2017 it was sitting at a hefty 743 kilograms, and belonged to New South Wales grower Dale Oliver.

But he's also got an agenda. He wants as many people as possible to take up his scientific methods for better results on a broader scale.

'At the end of the day, for me, people do not listen to what I'm trying to convey,' he says. 'People of my dad's generation, they have used all these synthetic fertilisers. They are pushing all the figures in the wrong directions, and it's just doing a terrible job with our soils for future generations. I guess no one listens until you can prove it. The only time people will listen will be when, "Wow, Newitt's grown a 1000-kilogram pumpkin. How did he do that?" And then they'll stand up and listen to you.'

It's proving a costly hobby. He spends 'well and truly more' than he takes home each year with a $500 Bream Creek Show win.

'When I first started out, it wasn't so bad, but you understand when you don't have the right climate like we have, it's tough here, you have to start making things and making your own microclimates. The cost starts to escalate,' he says.

The giant pumpkins aren't even really for eating.

'You can, if you get a good one which is hard in the flesh and deep,' he says. 'You have to understand, there's eight to ten inches through the walls. There's a lot of pulp. It makes a lot of pulpy product.

'It's just a matter of adding sweet potato, garlic and onion and you can make quite a nice brew from it, but they're not an eating pumpkin as such, no.'

Last time, he carved off a 150-kilogram chunk of pumpkin which fed half of the town.

'I just cut a big slab off and carried it into the bank, whatever you could lift. They can share it among themselves,' he says.

'It was priceless to see the look on their faces. Their jaws were dragging on the ground. It was one big slab of pumpkin.'

The cement watchdog is barking.

'Watch the corner as it comes away from the pumpkin,' Shane directs.

It's show day eve, and harvest time. Shane and two men are attempting to move the massive pumpkin onto a pallet to take it to the weigh-off. They've removed the steel-and-sheet canopy from overhead.

'Pull it straight up,' he says.

A harness is placed around the mass, and a large tractor brought in for the extraction. Shane slashes through the thick vines with a knife.

'Just go gently. Real steady. Watch it.'

With a nod, the driver reverses the tractor, lifting the pallet and the pumpkin up over onto a ute parked nearby.

'At the end of the day, after six months, it's very rewarding. If you can get there safely,' Shane says. 'That's what it's all about. Getting to the scales in one piece.'

Shane's feeling much more upbeat than he was, as he brushes the pumpkin down with a white cloth.

'She's looking much better than I thought,' he says. 'She might have a chance.'

The next day, pallets are grouped together in a paddock at the Bream Creek Show, adjacent to a pallet of giant zucchinis. At the other end of the grounds, a marching band of bag pipes is performing.

Shane confides to another grower that he's feeling a little anxious. He wants to beat his personal best from last year's show – 422.5 kilograms. 'That's how you improve,' he says.

One by one, the pumpkins are lifted onto the large, flat, square scales. The smallest go first.

'49.5 kilograms.'

As they are weighed, a steward writes the weight on the now-hardened skin with a black marker pen.

Shane's 'Terminator' is the biggest pumpkin there.

'Anybody want to take a guess?' the compere says, as it is lifted to be weighed.

'860,' says a voice from the crowd, gathered behind a fence.

'431,' says another.

It's lowered onto the scales.

'Whoop. He's done it. 424.5! He's beaten his previous record by a couple of kilos. Well done. Great effort.'

The crowd applauds, and Shane is ecstatic.

'I didn't think we'd get the old record. I didn't think she'd do it. But we have,' he says. 'We'll let her have a bit of peace now; let her sit for a day or two at home before we'll cut her open and harvest the seeds. Then we'll try and make a bit of soup for ourselves and share her around the community.'

Then it's back to the drawing board to start the growing process all over again.

'Once you reach the top there's only one way to go, and that's down,' he says. 'If someone gets a personal best one day I'm bound to be rolled. It's inevitable. I'll say congratulations to them because they will have earned it.'

24

Cygnet

Location: 54 km south of Hobart.

Population: 929

Aired: *Back Roads* travelled to Cygnet in its second season.
The episode aired in January 2017.

HELEN THOMSON IS CROUCHING over a bright-pink laundry bucket, mixing up lime putty. She breaks up pieces of what looks like sheep's wool and adds them to the mix, which she sloshes around in the bucket, stirring it thoroughly with a trowel. She's hard at work in the backyard of a large straw bale house in Cygnet, in the rolling green hills of the Huon Valley, south of Hobart.

It's a gorgeous October day. The sun has taken the sting out of the air. It's almost warm. For Tasmania, anyway.

Helen's been waiting to do this job for a while. And finally the weather has acquiesced. Her grey hair is tied back in a bun and she's wearing long black rubber gloves. She has a hawk tool in one hand and a plasterer's float in the other. Helen loads a tool with some of the slurry and straightens up. Then she presses the putty onto the outside wall of the house, firmly, but gently, scraping upwards, again and again until it is smooth. She steps back to critique her work. Satisfied, she turns around to the breathtaking vista and takes a moment. Then she breaks out in song.

'Oh, how I love my tea, tea in the afternoon,' she sings in an operatic soprano. 'I can't do without it. So I think I'll have another cup verrrr–eh–herr-re-y soon.'

She's doing it all for the cameras, of course. *Back Roads* has come to visit. It's October 2016. But if you closed your eyes, the harmony wouldn't be out of place in a fancy concert hall.

The notes echo out over the landscape, a pretty combination of mottled greens: grasses, shrubs and trees. The Huon Valley used to be covered in apple orchards. Today, as city folk and mainlanders have moved into the small town, they've transformed into grassy paddocks, for hobby farms and bountiful grazing country. A bird whistles nearby as if in competition with the melody. There are mountains in the distance.

'Tell you what, it's a tough job, this. Particularly the scenery, it's awful,' Helen laughs. 'The thing I always find amazing, and I've been here five years now and I still haven't got my head around it, is the locals don't think you have a view unless you see water. Well, this is pretty okay too, you know.'

Back Roads has come to film Helen at work in her straw bale rendering business. She's done a deal with the house owner – she's repairing the outside wall in exchange for some frozen grass-fed beef.

'I got as far as the second coat. Obviously, in order to have the best possible result we've got to let that dry first,' she tells him.

Helen's a natural builder. Five years ago she was a classical soprano in Europe, living with her wife, Chloe, in the Netherlands. She loved her work as a freelance soloist, part-time with the Netherlands Radio Choir, and part-time as a freelance soloist and ensemble member. But the lifestyle was a challenge.

'It was very crowded, terrible weather, lots of congestion, very little access to wilderness; very hard to live any kind of life that's close to the earth,' she says. 'It was hard to get proper food – hard to live well in general, as compared to Australia generally and Tasmania particularly. 'It's just really easy to live well here by comparison. It was a lifestyle versus career kind of choice.'

Over time the couple talked about returning home to Australia, to practice sustainability and live off-grid.

'It's a classic tree-change story, really,' Helen says. 'My partner and I started having a conversation about how the world was going to hell in a handcart and we had a big think about what it was that we could and wanted to do about that. We thought that perhaps some sort of leading by example would be a good thing.'

They knew what they wanted. Some acreage, left largely untouched so that 'little wild things could be there'. They wanted to be self-sufficient. To grow vegies. To reduce their carbon footprint on the world. But their skills when they started were 'fairly limited', Helen recalls.

'So the first thing we did was get educated and then we bought a parcel of land here in the region and did the whole tree-change thing,' she says. 'And we went from being respectively a professional gardener and professional singer to being professional earth builders.'

It's been a steep learning curve. One of the first lessons was learning to ask for help from neighbours.

'I remember a couple of years ago we left the road. We were driving down Tobys Hill Road with a trailer on the back. We met somebody on the wrong side of the road coming up. We braked; the trailer jack knifed – you know, it's a typical story – we left the road slowly and nobody got hurt, and the car didn't even get particularly badly damaged but it was off the road and we needed to get back on the road, so of course we called a tow truck, as you do.

'It was Christmas Eve so it took half a day and the tow truck had to come from Eastern Shore. It cost a fortune. It was an enormous faff and very annoying.

'Afterwards we went to our neighbouring farmer and we were telling him about it and he's like, "Ah, I've got a tractor, why didn't you call me? I could have got you back on the road in 20 minutes". It's like, oh, okay; lesson learned. You look to your neighbour first and then you look to their friends and then you look to their friends, and after that you maybe call in a professional.'

*

Helen has well and truly learned many lessons from her tree-change move to regional Tasmania. But 18 months after *Back Roads*' visit, she's in a very different place, physically and mentally.

'It was odd, primarily because by the time the filming had happened my story was already in the process of changing quite comprehensively,' she says. 'We did the preliminary interviews a fair bit earlier than the filming. Between the preliminary interviews and the filming I'd stopped doing fieldwork because I'd had a back injury.'

Her domestic situation was also changing.

'That whole scenario was pretty weird. Not knowing what was going to happen next.'

Before the couple moved to Cygnet, music had played a central role in Helen's life. In some ways it was almost predestined – her parents, Val and Julian, had met in a university choir in Canberra.

Helen was singing in a choir herself by the age of four, and under the tutelage of music educator Judith Clingan, who was trained in Hungary, she developed a solid and comprehensive base of musical knowledge from which to grow.

And she's been hearing musical notes in her head as long as she can remember. Helen says her music brain is very much like a science brain.

'I am extremely analytical,' she says. 'I see patterns and that informs my practice as a musician and also as a composer.'

When Helen and Chloe moved back to Australia from overseas, Helen was certain music wasn't going to be a part of her future story. She was quite prepared to walk away from her talent, which a little part of her brain considered a self-indulgence.

'I wasn't planning on being a professional musician when I got here. I was planning on being a hobbyist,' she says. 'And dagging around with a few mates and singing a bit of folk, and otherwise just hanging up my harp.

'I was going to do natural building and be a resilience educator, and I was going to do singing in my free time.'

It was a conscious decision.

'I felt like I had a responsibility to do something a bit more environmentally friendly,' she says. 'My partner and I saw an opportunity to make a not-insignificant impact, particularly on people with challenges: a low income or younger people who needed skills. We were hoping to have an impact on that sector of the market for resilience skills training. Things didn't work out the way we were hoping.'

They were doing backbreaking work. And not really earning enough money to survive.

Then the musical opportunities started seeping in, one by one, until they snowballed into an incredible performance at Hobart's Theatre Royal in April 2018.

In 2012, at a birthday party, Hobart-based artist and singer-songwriter Deb Wace asked Helen if she would direct a queer choir. Then Cygnet-based community arts worker Gai Anderson asked her if she would set up a choir in Cygnet.

'We fell straight into a musical community as soon as we arrived – we kind of were in this folk circle that was meeting for a session once a week and it was like being surrounded by family suddenly,' Helen says.

Helen is in a local baroque group. When she performs in Hobart, she presents the same concert in Cygnet.

'People come to stuff here, they really do – they show up in force. It's pretty easy to get a decent audience for just about anything. People are intrepid and interested and curious and want to support culture, so it's actually a really vibrant cultural landscape, this, as well. There's all sorts of talent in the hills. It's great.'

She didn't know it then, but it was all building up to something quite special. By early 2015, Helen was working in vocal coaching, performing, directing and composing. Then one day, out of the blue, she decided she wanted to write a double choir requiem.

'I was pretty arrested by that idea. As an early music practitioner I've done a lot of excellent double choir work from the 1700s,' she says. 'I've also done a fair bit of fairly interesting work with early brass, where one of the choirs is a brass and the other is a vocal choir.

'I started talking about the possibility of incorporating local poetry.'

She was talking it over with Hobart arts worker Frances Butler, a friend from choir, over a glass of wine.

'Eventually this little silence falls. Well, if you are going to do it from a local angle, says Frances, why wouldn't you do it in language?' Helen says. 'Tasmanian Aboriginal language.'

'That was the moment where the idea grew a million legs. It stopped being this kind of ridiculous blue-sky conversation that meant nothing and suddenly became this thing that absolutely needed to be done immediately.'

And so Helen's life shifted into an inherently complex, fraught and enormously rewarding world. Over the next three years, working with Frances in partnership with local Aboriginal creatives Greg Lehman, Julie Gough and Jim Everett-puralia meenamatta, they would write, compose and perform a groundbreaking 84-minute rite of mourning for the terrible legacies of the Black War. *A Tasmanian Requiem* is only the second double choir requiem in the world.

'It's about the Black War and its legacy, and about the loss that every single person on this island suffered, and suffers now, as a result,' Helen says. 'The generational echoes for everybody, for the fact there was an attempted genocide here. And it's also about the fact there's been a pretty horrifying and continuing agenda of enforced forgetting. It was a huge libretto to write.'

The work is full of grief. And remorse. Foreboding. Moments of joy. Regret. It melds words from the Latin Mass for the Dead with original poetry in Tasmanian Aboriginal language and English, and projections on a cinema screen. It wasn't any wonder Helen had trouble sleeping: the part she sang – voicing the horror of the period – was nauseating.

'Interpreting that work, I wouldn't outsource that to my worst enemy,' she says. 'It's not the sort of work you make other people do. It's too horrible.'

As the production gathered pace, she admits to feeling a bit manic. Madly rushing around. Ocean swimming to calm down. The adrenalin stuck with her for a month after the event, which received wide acclaim.

She's come full circle as a musician now. She admits it's a relief to be finally embracing the practice again. Though she hasn't given up on her sustainable living ambitions either. She's picked up work teaching classical vocals at the University of Tasmania's Conservatorium of Music, and solo gigs on the mainland and with the Tasmanian Symphony Orchestra.

'It's like a homecoming,' she says. 'If I'm not doing music I don't feel like I'm in integrity with myself.'

She's already thinking up new projects and new ways to encourage people to live more environmentally aware.

'I have in the back of my mind another idea,' she smiles.

She wants to form a collective of people to build tiny houses on wheels.

'I do think that change is going to happen from the bottom up,' she says. 'Advocacy is something I'm reasonably interested in.

'I do want to make good things. I don't think I'm just being self-indulgent by wanting to make music. I want to make music that makes a change.'

It's important to her that the music has meaning. After all, music is one of the most powerful mediums around.

'I don't just want to do it because it's the thing I'm best at by far. I want to do it because it's a vehicle for change; it's a vehicle for getting in at the heart level, where intellect isn't going to necessarily get the job done.'

Acknowledgements

Thanks to each and every one of the people whose stories make up this book, for their generosity, firstly during the filming for *Back Roads*, and secondly for sharing their stories with me so openly and enthusiastically, even in the face of my pesky pedantry with the facts. And to those behind the scenes who helped bring this book to fruition, including the many experts who provided invaluable assistance. Everyone has a story, and hearing extraordinary tales from people and communities across remote and regional Australia, who often didn't think theirs was anything special, has been one of my most cherished parts of producing *Back Roads* programs. Thanks also to the enduring *Back Roads* team, particularly executive producer Brigid Donovan, and supervising producer Kerri Ritchie, whose support and belief in me has been unshakable. And to Heather Ewart, without whom none of us would have set out on this incredible journey. – Karen Michelmore